Last Will and Testament

Protect Your Loved Ones

A
Step-by-Step Guide
to Do-It-Yourself

LawPak's Commitment and Goal

The goal of LawPak is to simplify legal information for consumers. Our LawPak's are designed to contain accurate, easy-to-read information and forms. However, no publication can take the place of a competent professional.

LawPak is committed to designing the highest quality forms and guides. We believe that non-lawyers should have access to legal information that has been researched and professionally prepared. Our publications can save the non-lawyer unnecessary legal expenses by providing information to better understand their legal problem.

However, we cannot guarantee that the way you complete the forms or that the information given will be totally accurate for and pertinent to your particular circumstances. Please be aware that laws, regulations and procedures are constantly changing and may be subject to differing interpretations.

We will guarantee that we have used extensive efforts to provide you with clear instructions and forms so that you may have the opportunity to learn about legal procedures and handle your own legal matters if you choose to do so. In order to constantly improve our legal forms and LawPaks, we welcome your suggestions and comments.

 *The LawPak Publishing Professionals*

Words for Thought

"Censorship comes from the rulers' fears and the zealots' belief in the single truth: the only religion, the only system, the only morality."
A.M. Rosenthal

"Education is a private matter between the person and the world of knowledge and experience. It has little to do with school or college."
Lillian Smith

This LawPak publication may not be copied, transmitted, transcribed, stored in a retrieval system, or translated into any human or computer language, in any form or by any means, electronic, mechanical, magnetic, chemical, manual or otherwise, without written permission of the publisher, except that the forms may be photocopied or reproduced by the purchaser for their own use, but not for resale. This publication is intended to be utilized by the purchaser for their own benefit, and the use of this publication to benefit a second party may be considered unauthorized practice of law.

LIMITED WARRANTY AND DISCLAIMER

LAWPAK INC. MAKES NO REPRESENTATIONS OR WARRANTIES WITH RESPECT TO THE CONTENT HEREOF AND SPECIFICALLY DISCLAIMS ANY IMPLIED WARRANTIES OR MERCHANTABILITY OR FITNESS FOR ANY PARTICULAR PURPOSE. IT IS UNDERSTOOD THAT BY USING THIS PUBLICATION, THE PURCHASER IS ACTING AS THEIR OWN ATTORNEY.

Although care has been taken to ensure the accuracy and utility of the information and forms contained in this publication, it is understood by all parties that neither LawPak, the authors, the retailers, nor the distributors assume any liability or responsibility to anyone for loss or damage caused or alleged to be caused by the use of the information or forms contained in this publication. The liability of LawPak, the retailers or the distributors shall not exceed the purchase price of this publication. The use of this publication constitutes acceptance of the above terms. LawPak, Inc., reserves the right to revise this publication and to make changes from time to time in its content without the obligation to notify any person or organization of such revisions or changes.

This publication is designed to provide accurate and authoritative information in regard to the subject matter covered. It is sold with the understanding that the publisher is not engaged in rendering legal, accounting, or any other professional service. If legal advice or other expert assistance is required, the services of a competent professional person should be sought.

From the Declaration of Principles jointly adopted by a Committee of the American Bar Association and a Committee of Publishers and Associations.

Table of Contents

A. **Introduction** 7

    A1 - About LawPak

    A2 - Why Do I Need a Will

    A3 - Finding an Attorney

    A4 - Condition For a Last Will and Testament

    A5 - Technical Requirements For a Valid Will

    A6 - Forms Needed For Doing Your Own Last Will and Testament

    A7 - Commonly Asked Questions

    A8 - What Cannot Be Accomplished in a Will

B. **Making Your Last Will and Testament** 17

    B1 - General Information

    B2 - Who Can Use LawPak's Will Forms

    B3 - Special State Requirements

C. **LawPak's Will Provisions** 21

    C 1 - Your Name

    C2 - Your Address

    C3 - Heirs and Beneficiaries

    C4 - Executors

    C5 - Appointing Guardians

    C6 - Signing Your Will

    C7 - Witnesses

    C8 - Notary Public

    C9 - What Should I Do With My Will When Completed

D. **Making and Typing the Complete Will Yourself** 33

    D1 - General Information

    D2 - Mandatory and Optional Provision

    D3 - Other Optional Provisions

E. The Probate Process 43

E1 - Introduction

E2 - The Steps in the Probate Process

E3 - Advantages and Disadvantages of Probate

E4 - Estate Taxes

F. Organizing Your Estate 49

F1 - Checklist for Immediate Action

F2 - Financial Power of Attorney

F3 - Living Will

F4 - Funeral Arrangements

F5 - Letter of Instruction

Forms and Checklists

· Biographical Information (husband and wife)

· Funeral Arrangements (husband and wife)

· Safe Deposit Box Contents

· Document Location and Records

· Other Personal Records

Blank Forms with Samples for a Last Will and Testament 61

Last Will and Testament Without Minor Children

Last Will and Testament With Minor Children

Last Will and Testament to Make and Type Yourself

Appendix 113

Checklist to Complete a Last Will and Testament

Explanation of Terms

Return Card to LawPak for Updates

Order Form for Other LawPak Publications

CHAPTER A
Introduction

A1 About This LawPak

The intent of this LawPak is to assist you in writing a Last Will and Testament. However, you may use a LawPak as one of many source materials to help you gain a better understanding of your legal needs and still decide to consult with an attorney. This LawPak is written in easy-to-understand language and addresses the most common questions and procedures concerning the way to draft a Last Will and Testament.

LawPak, Inc., is, however, a publishing company and, as such, does not attempt to form opinions, offer solutions or give legal advice concerning any aspect of your particular situation. The opinions expressed in this book are those of the authors and should not be interpreted as representing those of the entire legal community.

Throughout this LawPak, you are advised of situations when you *should* speak with a lawyer. Consult a lawyer if you have **any** doubts or questions about any matters, including anything discussed in LawPak. It should be noted that certain situations *require* professional legal assistance.

If you have decided that you can and should draft your own Last Will and Testament, you should read this *entire* book before doing anything. It is written in plain language, but read it *carefully*. Do not do anything unless you fully understand what you want to accomplish.

A2 Why Do I Need a Will?

You have purchased this book because you have some understanding of the need for everyone to have a will. Every adult should have a will, but most neglect to prepare one because of the cost of legal service, simple inconvenience, or a failure to understand the necessity of drafting a will. If you do not have a will, the state – not you – will decide who inherits your property and will choose guardians for your children based on state statutes of Descent and Distribution (laws). When a person dies intestate (without a will), the legal system that distributes that person's property does not consider the needs of individuals. The laws are written for general application and not to suit an individual's personal interests or goals. With a Last Will and Testament, *you* decide, according to your wishes, how your estate will be distributed. A will can ensure that your wishes are carried out and prevent confusion and feuding over your estate.

You should not think that your spouse will automatically inherit your property if you should die without a will. Without a will, your spouse will inherit only one-third to one-half of your estate depending upon your state law. The remainder will go to other relatives although this may not represent your choice. After your death, your intentions about the disposition of your property has no legal support unless you take the time now to prepare your Last Will and Testament.

You and your spouse should execute *two separate* wills and use *two separate* original forms (not photocopies). It is *not* advisable to have a joint will. Each individual should have his or her own personal will. A joint will may cause major problems when an estate is probated at death. This LawPak contains *one* Last Will and Testament form for a person with minor children and *one* form for a person with no minor children. Either can be used by one married, single or divorced individual.

We suggest you remove the forms (they are perforated) and photocopy them before you type the necessary information in the blank forms. Use the extra set as worksheets until you have a completed a final draft to be typed. The law does not permit any corrections, crossing out, or erasing of anything contained in the original draft of your will. It must be a *perfect* copy. Remember to destroy your worksheets after you have completed your final draft.

You may want to review your final draft with a lawyer to make sure the will conforms to your wishes and to state requirements.

A3 Finding an Attorney

LawPaks are not written to replace lawyers. They are intended to give you a basic understanding of your legal situation and offer an affordable option to those individuals who decide they can do certain legal procedures themselves. You must decide if or when the services of a lawyer may be necessary for your circumstances.

There are no laws which require you to hire a lawyer to represent you or sign your legal documents. When you represent yourself, you are said to be acting propia persona ("pro per"), which is Latin for "yourself."

If you have a problem with some part of your Last Will and Testament or need additional information, you may decide that a conference with a lawyer would be beneficial. Instead of having the attorney do the complete Last Will and Testament, you might seek assistance with only part of it. Many attorneys may not be willing to assist you with just a part of the will so you may have to call several until you find one who is responsive to the idea.

The best way to find an attorney is through a trusted person who has had a satisfactory experience with one. When you call an attorney, don't be intimidated. Ask what their fees would be for a Last Will and Testament and how much an initial interview will cost. Attorney fees will vary considerably. Most lawyers will do the first interview for $20 to $30. Hourly rates run from $85 to $300 per hour; a fee of $100 to $150 is fairly common for a Last Will and Testament.

Before you go to see an attorney, be sure you know exactly what you expect from their services. Have all relevant documents and information with you. As we just mentioned, most attorneys work and charge for their services based upon an hourly rate.

Many federally funded legal aid offices, which were created to assist people with low incomes at no charge, *will not* normally help you with a Last Will and Testament because these types of documents are "fee generating." This means that the legal community objects to Legal Aid handling for free this type of case which could generate a fee to a lawyer working outside of Legal Aid.

A4 Conditions For a Last Will and Testament

This LawPak explains who can write a Last Will and Testament, what forms are needed and how to fill out and file the forms. It will also explain who you should tell about your Last Will and Testament and where you should place it for safekeeping.

In order for you to do your own Last Will and Testament with this LawPak, you must meet **ALL** the following requirements:

◆ You must be at least eighteen years of age in almost all states (fourteen in Georgia).

◆ You must be competent (that is, legally sane).

◆ You must not be under any restraint (forced to write your Last Will and Testament in a certain manner).

◆ You must consider the state in which you make your will your place of legal residence.

◆ You must have at least two witnesses (some states require three witnesses) who are not named in your Last Will and Testament watch you sign your Last Will and Testament. They must *see* you sign, and they must see each other sign as witnesses.

◆ You must decide who you want to inherit your property.

◆ If you have minor children, you must decide who you want to take care of the children and their property.

If you cannot meet all of the above requirements, you will not be able to do your own Last Will and Testament.

A5 Technical Requirements for a Valid Will

For a will to be valid, it must comply with the drafting requirements of state law. Generally, these requirements are less complex than many people think and are similar in all states. Lawyers prepare wills using a standard will form book, which is usually input into a word-processing system. They type in your name and the names of your beneficiaries, choose other standard provisions and information (legalese), and print your will. The following are the drafting requirements for a valid will:

◆ Your will *should be typewritten* and state expressly that it is your will. Oral wills or nuncupative wills are valid in only a few states and then only in special circumstances such as immediate danger of death (war). The handwritten will, or holographic will, is recognized in twenty-five states, but it is difficult to probate because it usually is not witnessed; this makes it necessary to prove that the will was written in the deceased person's handwriting.

◆ You must appoint at least one person who is responsible for the distribution of your property and the payment of your debts, etc. This person will act as your executor.

◆ The will must have at least one substantive provision (paragraph or clause): a provision making gifts of all or some of your property and/or a paragraph which appoints a guardian for your children.

◆ You must date and sign the will.

◆ Your will must be witnessed by at least two witnesses; some states require at least three witnesses. The witnesses must not inherit anything in the will. Witness requirements are covered in detail in the following chapters.

The above list shows the basic technical requirements for a valid will. For your will to be legal and valid, it:

◆ does not have to be prepared, approved, or signed by a lawyer.

◆ does not have to be notarized.

◆ does not have to be filed or recorded with any government agency.

A6 Forms Needed for Doing Your Own Last Will and Testament

Our Last Will and Testament packet contains the forms you need to do your own Last Will and Testament. The forms will help you provide for dividing your property after your death and appoint a guardian to care for your minor children. They can also help you name the person who will distribute your property, and provide that the person so named be permitted to serve without posting a bond after your death.

> NOTE: This LawPak contains the blank forms for TWO different wills. One set of blank forms contains a clause to appoint a guardian for minor children; the other set does not contain a guardianship clause.

The contents of the forms and how to fill them out will be explained in detail in the following sections.

A7 Commonly Asked Questions

What protection does a Last Will and Testament provide?

It can keep the State from determining who gets your property, can prevent your spouse or heirs from posting an expensive bond, and, if you have children, can allow you the freedom to choose the guardian so the State does not take responsibility for appointing one.

What is the spouse entitled to without a Last Will and Testament?

This depends on whether the surviving spouse is the natural or adoptive parent of the child/children of the person who has died. This can become very complicated if you or your spouse has been previously married.

Can my spouse and I have one Last Will and Testament for both of us?

No. You and your spouse should each have your own Last Will and Testament. You should not have one Last Will and Testament for two people (a joint will).

Is it important to record my Last Will and Testament?

No, it is up to each individual to decide if this is necessary. Some people like to record their last Will and Testament so they know the county in which they reside has a record that a Last Will and Testament has been made. It is not necessary to record your Last Will and Testament to make it legal. Some states (Ohio and Texas) will store your will for a small fee.

How long will it take to write my Last Will and Testament?

It will take you as long as it takes to read this packet, make some very important decisions, and type in the blanks on your LawPak Last Will and Testament form or completely type your whole will yourself.

When I have completed my LawPak Last Will and Testament, do I have to go to Court or to a lawyer to have it reviewed?

No. However, if you would feel more comfortable, you can have it reviewed by a lawyer.

How many witnesses will I need?

At least two. A few states require three (see listing in Section C7).

How old must the witnesses be?

They must be at least 18 (eighteen) years of age and must be considered by state law to be a legally competent adult.

Do I have to supply addresses for all the beneficiaries, executors and guardians named in my will?

No, it is not required. However, supplying addresses offers a practical advantage by making it easier to locate and notify persons in the event of your death. You do not need to redo your will if their addresses change.

Do I have to let my witnesses read my Last Will and Testament?

No, they are only witnessing your *signature*, not the contents of the Last Will and Testament.

Do the people I choose have to be relatives?

No, just people you feel are trustworthy and would carry out your wishes.

Can a non-U.S. citizen inherit my property?

Yes.

What if I already have a Last Will and Testament and I wrote on it?

You should make a new Last Will and Testament because the Court will have no way of determining who made the changes or when they were made.

Once I make a Last Will and Testament, can I change it later?

Yes you can change it as many times as you wish. Each time you change it, you should make a *new* Last Will and Testament. Remember to tear up or destroy your old Last Will and Testament.

If I name someone in my Last Will and Testament to serve as a guardian or executor/trix and that person does not want to serve, what will happen?

That person will not have to serve, which is why we recommend picking an alternate. If you do not provide for an alternate the Court will appoint someone.

Should my witnesses be people named in the Last Will and Testament?

Absolutely not. Choose two or three people who are not named in the Last Will and Testament as heirs/beneficiaries, executors, or guardians.

Does my State recognize Last Will and Testaments from other states?

Usually, if the Last Will and Testament conforms to State standards and requirements.

What is an executor or executrix?

An executor or executrix is the person who carries out the wishes of the deceased. An executor is male; an executrix is female.

What does "without bond" mean?

"Without Bond" means that you trust a person enough to distribute your property or watch your children and/or their money without requiring that the person post a bond. If you do require the executor/trix to post a bond and he or she misuses the funds from your estate, the bonding company will pay your heirs.

Do most people allow their executor/trix to serve without bond?

Yes, because most people pick someone they trust to distribute their estate. However, if you have no close friends or relatives, you may want to make the appointed executor/trix post a bond. That person will be reimbursed for the cost of the bond by the estate at a later time.

What factors should be used in choosing an executor/trix?

In choosing an executor/trix, you should pick someone you consider to be fair and levelheaded. Choose a person who has the time to go to a lawyer's office and sign all the necessary papers to have your estate administered.

What factors should be used in choosing a guardian for my children?

You should choose a person who would not object to raising your children if something happened to you. Before you name someone to be the guardian of your children, make sure you ask that person in advance so that if the guardian is called upon to serve, he or she will not be surprised by the responsibility of raising your child/ren.

If my parents are elderly, can I still appoint them as guardians for my children in my Last Will and Testament?

Yes, there is no age limitation. However, we recommend that you also choose someone who is younger as an alternate in case your parents should die.

A8 What Cannot Be Accomplished in a Will

You can give away your property within your will in almost any way you desire. You can leave it to your family, church, grandchildren, lodge, foundation, or college. You can give it to non-citizens, and you can disinherit anyone you want except your spouse.

There are, however, some limitations as to what your will can accomplish:

◆ You cannot use a will to leave money for an illegal purpose.

◆ You cannot legally bind your executor to hire any particular attorney to probate your estate.

◆ You cannot make a gift contingent to require, restrain or encourage certain types of behavior on the part of a recipient, such as divorce, marriage, or change of religion.

◆ You must own the property which you are giving away in the will at the time of your death. If you sell or give away any property which you have mentioned in your will, you should update your will.

◆ You cannot give away property in a will which you have legally transferred by other means such as proceeds from life insurance or individual retirement accounts (IRA).

Chapter B
Making Your Last Will and Testament

B1 General Information

The most important and difficult aspect of doing your own Last Will and Testament is deciding who you want to receive your property, who you want to care for your children, who you want to administer your estate, and who will properly attest (witness and sign) the will.

Generally, you cannot disinherit your spouse. This means that as long as you are legally married to someone (no divorce or dissolution of the marriage has been declared by the Court), your spouse can always elect to take against the will. In simple terms, the spouse could choose to take that to which he or she would be entitled to under state law if you did not have a will. This is true even if you make a Last Will and Testament. (See Section B3.)

You can disinherit anyone **except** a spouse. It is not unusual for a family member – for example, an adult child – who has been disinherited to initiate legal action to try to modify the property distribution of a will. This kind of action can be minimized if the will clearly states the intent of the person making will (testator) and provides a *token payment* to the relative who may have strong feelings concerning the distribution of your property. In this manner, the Court knows that you have not accidentally forgotten to provide for the person in the will. It is better to leave a wayward adult child $20.00 than have your will subject to an expensive lawsuit.

LawPak has included provisions for you to make *two specific bequests* of personal property within the blank forms. A specific bequest means you want to leave a particular item (i.e., a piece of jewelry or other valuable) to a particular person. You may, for example, want to leave your mother's ring to your daughter or your father's watch to your son. Within the language of the provision, you must be precise in describing the particular item(s) in order to avoid confusion concerning your intent.

In addition, this LawPak contains provisions for you to make *two general bequests*. A general bequest is personal property paid to a beneficiary out of your general estate and not a specific item. A general bequest is usually in the form of money.

If you wish to leave more than two specific or general bequests or no bequest, and/or wish to leave specific real property (real estate, buildings, land) to specific beneficiaries, you should draft your will using our second drafting method; that is, you should type the *entire* contents of your Last Will and Testament. A sample form is included in this LawPak to assist you. Note that we provide the wording for the *mandatory* provisions and you select those *optional* provisions which fit your particular circumstances (such as adding additional bequests).

There are some situations when you should consider consulting a lawyer regarding the drafting of your will. You should consult a lawyer:

◆ if you are separated from your spouse and not yet legally divorced.

◆ if you have a child who is mentally and/or physically handicapped.

◆ if you want to create an extensive trust for your children or spouse.

◆ if there is a trust fund currently in existence for your personal benefit.

◆ if you think a member of your family will challenge your will.

B2 Who Can Use the LawPak Last Will and Testament Form

LawPak's forms can be used by any individual – married, single, divorced, or widowed – whether or not he or she has children under eighteen. However, we **strongly** recommend you consult an attorney to advise you if you and your spouse are *separated*.

B3 Special State Requirements

a Community Property Laws

Community Property Laws are state laws that provide for the joint ownership of property which is acquired during a marriage. It does not matter whether the property was acquired by both parties together or one party; the property is still Community Property unless one spouse has disclaimed an interest in the property by a proper deed.

The effect of this law makes it impossible for one spouse to will away the other spouse's interest in any property. The states which have Community Property Laws are as follows:

Arizona	**Louisiana**	**Texas**
California	**Nevada**	**Washington (State)**
Idaho	**New Mexico**	**Wisconsin**

b Curtesy Laws

Curtesy Laws were adopted by certain states to provide the *husband* with the legal right to use one-third or more of the deceased wife's real property for as long as he lives. This is provided that the husband did not sign the deed to the property when it was sold.

Those states who have Curtesy Laws are as follows:

Delaware	**Massachusetts**	**Vermont**
District of Columbia	**Ohio**	**Virginia**
Hawaii	**Rhode Island**	**West Virginia**
Kentucky	**Tennessee**	**Wisconsin**

c Dower Laws

Dower Laws were adopted by certain states to provide the *wife* with the legal right to use one-third or more of the deceased husband's real property for as long as she lives. This right applies even though the property was sold to a third party. This is provided that the wife did not sign the deed when the property was sold.

Alabama	**Kentucky**	**New Jersey**	**Tennessee**
Delaware	**Massachusetts**	**Ohio**	**Vermont**
Florida	**Michigan**	**Rhode Island**	**Virginia**
Hawaii	**Montana**	**South Carolina**	**West Virginia**
Wisconsin			

CHAPTER C
LawPak's Will Provisions

This chapter shows examples of how to fill out your Last Will and Testament with LawPak. You will notice from the examples that all provisions except your **name**, **address**, **beneficiaries**, **executors** and **guardians** are already printed on your form. You need only type the missing information in the blanks, sign your name, date the form, and have your will witnessed by at least two (or three, if required) persons not named in the will to complete your LawPak Last Will and Testament.

C1 Your Name

When typing your name on your form, please use your **complete** name.

◆ Do not use a nickname.

◆ Use your middle name, not an initial.

◆ If you have no middle name, type nmn (no middle name).

Be sure you spell out your full first name, even if people call you by a shortened version of the name that appears on your birth certificate. For example, if your first name is Joseph, spell out the name "Joseph"; do not substitute "Joe."

Examples:

I, **JOSEPH ALLEN JONES**, now domiciled in <u>Your County, Your State</u>, do make, publish and declare this to be my Last Will and Testament, hereby revoking any and all Wills and Codicils heretofore made by me.

I, **JOHN MICHAEL DOE**, now domiciled in <u>Your County, Your State</u>, do make, publish and declare this to be my Last Will and Testament, hereby revoking any and all Wills and Codicils heretofore made by me.

I, **MARY nmn DOE**, now domiciled in <u>Your County, Your State</u>, do make, publish and declare this to be my Last Will and Testament, hereby revoking any and all Wills and Codicils heretofore made by me.

If your birth certificate has one name (i.e., Joseph Allen Jones) and you use a different name (i.e., Allen Jones), be sure to type in your given name and also aka (also known as) and the name you currently use. However, if you are married and are using your spouse's name, there is no need to use aka.

Example:

I, **JOSEPH ALLEN JONES, aka ALLEN JONES**, now domiciled in <u>Your County, Your State</u>, do make, publish and declare this to be my Last Will and Testament, hereby revoking any and all Wills and Codicils heretofore made by me.

C2 Address Provision

After you have typed your name in the space provided, type in the name of the county which you consider your permanent home.

Example:

I, JOHN MICHAEL DOE, now domiciled in **Montgomery County, Your State**, do make, publish and declare this to be my Last Will and Testament, hereby revoking any and all Wills and Codicils heretofore made by me.

C3 Beneficiary Provisions

The term "heirs" applies to those persons who would be entitled to your estate if you were to die without a will. "Beneficiaries" are those persons to whom you *choose* to give your property after you are deceased. Your beneficiaries can include your spouse, children relatives, friends and/or any institution to whom you wish to leave your estate. When completing the paragraph on beneficiaries, you must include the full name and relationship of the beneficiary. You may leave your estate to any one person or to more than one person. (Though you may not disinherit your spouse.) You may divide it into equal or unequal parts. If you feel unsure about the manner in which you have divided your property, *consult an attorney.*

a Specific Bequests

If you own a particular item of personal property (not real property such as real estate) that you want to leave as a gift to a certain beneficiary, this provision will accomplish that goal. Avoid making shared gifts of the same property because this will cause problems concerning which beneficiary actually controls the gift. You should be precise in describing the gift to avoid confusion later, and you should choose an alternate beneficiary.

Example:

I give, devise, and bequeath of this my estate, to each of the below-named beneficiaries, specific gifts of personal property, as follows:

a) I give **my father's gold pocket watch which has been in my family for three generations and 1000 shares of XYZ Company common stock** to my **son, Edward Arnold Jones of 2007 Second Street, His City, His State**, or if s/he (it) fails to survive me by thirty (30) days, to my **son, Matthew Adam Jones of 6161 Maple Avenue, His City, His State**.

b) I give my **1958 Ford T-bird Serial Number 0344583 and 1000 shares of ABC Company common stock** to my **son, Matthew Adam Jones of 6161 Maple Avenue, His City, His State**, or if s/he (it) fails to survive me by thirty (30) days, to my **son, Edward Arnold Jones of 2007 Second Street, His City, His State**.

b General Bequests

General bequests are those gifts which are paid to beneficiaries out of your general estate — usually in the form of money. The bequest can be left to any person, church, college, organization or charity. If you give a gift to an organization, it is very important that you learn the exact name of the organization and make sure they are permitted to receive gifts. Also, many states have laws limiting the amount of a gift to an organization to one-third of your estate if you have a spouse and/or minor children.

Example:

THIRD: I give, devise and bequeath of this my estate, to the below-named beneficiaries, specific cash gifts, as follows:

a) I give **Five Thousand and zero cents** Dollars (**$5,000.00**) to my **college, The University for All** of **300 Education Avenue, Its City, Its State**, or if s/he (it) fails to survive me by thirty (30) days, to my **brother, Earl James Jones** of **10 Sunshine Blvd., His City, His State**.

b) I give **One Thousand and zero cents** Dollars (**$1,000.00**) to my **good friend, John Quincy Doe** of **8844 Goodtimes Avenue, His City, His State**, or if s/he (it) fails to survive me by thirty (30) days, to my **brother, Earl James Jones** of **10 Sunshine Blvd., His City, His State**.

This sample is intended to show what you need to complete in the paragraph concerning beneficiaries:

All the rest, residue and remainder of my estate, whether real, personal, and mixed, of whatever kind and nature, and wheresoever situated, including all property which I may acquire or become entitled to after the execution of this Will, remaining after payment of my debts and funeral expenses, I give, devise and bequeath to my **(FIRST CHOICE) relationship(s), legal name(s) of person(s)** of **address of person(s)**. In the event that the before-named person(s) has predeceased me or we both die as the result of a common disaster, then I give, devise and bequeath my estate to my **(SECOND CHOICE) relationship(s), legal name(s) of person(s)** of **address of person(s).**

The *first blank* is intended to be used for your *first beneficiary*; that means, the person/s you wish to receive your property when you die. You must first specify their relationship to you: husband, wife, daughter, son, friend, neighbor, etc. It can be more than one person, or it can be a thing (church, organization, etc.). After you type in the relationship, then you must type the complete name(s) of the person you have chosen as your beneficiary.

The *second blank* is intended to be used for your *second beneficiary*. If the person you named as your first beneficiary is already deceased when you die, your second beneficiary will receive your property. It can also be any person(s) or thing(s) you choose. You must also type the relationship of this (these) person(s) and then type in the name(s) completely.

Examples:

All the rest and remainder of my estate, whether real, personal, and mixed, of whatever kind and nature, and wherever situated, including all property which I may acquire or become entitled to after the executive of this Will, remaining after payment of my debts and funeral expenses, I give, devise and bequeath unto my **wife**, **Mary nmn Doe** of **883 Chester Road, Her City, Her State**. In the event that s/he (it) has predeceased me or we both die as the result of a common disaster, then I give, devise and bequeath my estate unto my **wife's child**, **Susan Jane Evans** of **1994 W. Third Avenue, Her City, Her State**.

All the rest and remainder of my estate, whether real, personal, and mixed, of whatever kind and nature, and wheresoever situated, including all property which I may acquire or become entitled to after the executive of this Will, remaining after payment of my debts and funeral expenses, I give, devise and bequeath unto my **husband**, **Harry David Doe** of **894 Winston Place, His City, His State**. In the event that s/he (it) has predeceased me or we both die as the result of a common disaster, then I give, devise and bequeath my estate unto my **children**, **John Harry Doe and Karen Beth Doe Smith** of **199 E. Winston Place, Their City, Their State**.

All the rest and remainder of my estate, whether real, personal, and mixed, of whatever kind and nature, and wheresoever situated, including all property which I may acquire or become entitled to after the executive of this Will, remaining after payment of my debts and funeral expenses, I give, devise and bequeath unto my **wife**, **Mary nmn Doe** of **883 Chester Road, Her City, Her State**. In the event that s/he (it) has predeceased me or we both die as the result of a common disaster, then I give, devise and bequeath my estate unto my **church**, **the Good Samaritan Church** of **9942 N. Hamilton Road, Its City, Its State**.

C4 Executors

The executor/trix is the person whom you appoint to take care of your final wishes, as expressed in your will. This person usually works with a lawyer to make sure that the directions in your Last Will and Testament are performed after your death.

Responsibilities of the Executor/trix

◆ To provide for the payment of your debts (from your estate).

◆ To divide the property in the manner which your will sets forth.

◆ To advise the lawyer/court as to what and where your assets are.

◆ To sell, by public or private sale, any or all your property after you are deceased.

◆ To make the decisions as to whether the claims made against your estate for any debts are valid claims.

◆ To make any decisions concerning the division of the property in the event your heirs cannot agree.

Who Should the Executor/trix Be?

◆ The Executor/trix may be any person over eighteen whom you choose and who you feel will be able to handle your affairs. It should be someone who is responsible.

◆ The person can be a relative or a friend.

◆ If you are married, the Executor/trix is usually your spouse. However, if your spouse is unable, for physical or mental reasons, to take care of the final distribution of your property, the Executor/trix can be any person over eighteen you choose.

◆ It is advisable to choose someone who is a resident of your state.

You can require that the executor/trix not be bonded if you feel the person you have chosen will be fair and honest in performing his or her duties. If, for any reason, you have any doubt about the executor's ability to handle the property and money of the estate, you may want to have the person bonded to protect the estate assets. Your LawPak Last Will and Testament form has a clause which states that *no* bond shall be required. If you feel a bond should be required, you *cannot* use the preprinted forms and should consult an attorney.

Your Executor/trix Provision needs to contain this paragraph:

I appoint my **relationship**, **name of first choice for executor** of **executor's address, city and state**, to be the Executor/trix of this my Last Will and Testament, to serve without bond. If s/he shall predecease me or, for any reason fail to qualify as an Executor/trix, then in such event, my **relationship**, **name of second choice**, of **alternate executor's address, city and state** shall be appointed Executor/trix to serve without bond.

When you fill out your Executor/trix Provision, note that the *first blank* is intended to be used for your *first executor/trix choice*; this is the person you wish to appoint to do all the duties described above to carry out your final wishes. The *second blank* is to be used to designate your *second choice of executor/trix*. If the person you named as your first choice is unable to serve for any reason, your second choice would administer your estate. Be sure to type in the relationship and the full name for both your first and second choices; you may supply their address.

Examples:

I appoint my **wife**, **Cynthia Davis Jones** of **33 Maple Avenue, Her City, Her State**, to be the Executor/trix of this my Last Will and Testament, to serve without bond. If s/he shall predecease me or, for any reason, fail to qualify as an Executor/trix, then in such event, my **son, Edward Arnold Smith** of **2007 Second Street, His City, His State**, shall be appointed Executrix to serve without bond.

I appoint my **wife**, **Cynthia Davis Jones** of **33 Maple Avenue, Her City, Her State**, to be the Executor/trix of this my Last Will and Testament, to serve without bond. If s/he shall predecease me or, for any reason, fail to qualify as an Executor/trix, then in such event, **my friend**, **Richard Howard Carter** of **224 Oak Street, His City, His State**, shall be appointed Executor to serve without bond.

C5 Appointing Guardians

If you have children under the age of eighteen, you will use the form for the Last Will and Testament with Minor Children. To complete it, read all of the previous paragraphs sections concerning the Will Without Minor Child/ren. You will follow the same procedure and provide all of the same information except that your Last Will and Testament will *also* include a paragraph providing for a guardian if you have children under eighteen. It is essential that you appoint someone, in your Last Will and Testament, to serve as the guardian of your child or children in the event you die before your children attain their majority. This person will have legal custody of your children until they reach the age of eighteen. *If you fail to appoint a guardian, the Court can choose any person it thinks is right and proper.*

If you and your child's/children's other parent are divorced, in the event of your death, the other parent has the right to be guardian of your child/ children. However, we still recommend naming an alternate guardian.

Duties of a Guardian

◆ To protect and control.

◆ To provide suitable living conditions.

◆ To provide a suitable education.

◆ To obey all the orders of the probate court concerning the distribution of money for the children.

◆ To keep the probate court advised on a timely basis as to the distribution of assets.

◆ To manage the estate in the best interest of your child/ren.

◆ To pay all debts and collect all debts due your child/ren.

◆ To obey all court orders.

◆ To file any lawsuit necessary for the child/ren.

There are, or course, many other practical, day-to-day duties a guardian must perform in caring for the child/ren. Therefore, when deciding on a suitable guardian, choose someone who has your utmost confidence and trust.

The Last Will and Testament With Minor Children contains the necessary Guardian Provision for you to complete to appoint your guardian. The *first blank* in the clause is intended to be used for your *first choice*. This is the person you appoint, in the event of your death, to serve as guardian of your minor children and perform all the duties described above. The *second blank* is intended to used for your *second choice* of guardian. If the person you named as your first choice is unable to serve for any reason, your second guardian choice would become the guardian of your children. For both the first and second choices, type the person's relationship to you (husband, wife, son, daughter, friend, neighbor, etc.). Then type the person's *full name*. You may add the address.

Examples:

I designate and appoint my **brother**, **Earl James Smith** of **10 Sunshine Blvd., His City, His State**, of as the Guardian of the person and estate of my minor child/ren. In the event that the above-appointed Guardian shall not be able to serve as Guardian for any reason, I designate and appoint my **friend**, **Richard James Carter** of **224 Oak Street, His City, His State**, as the Guardian of the person and estate of my minor child/ren.

I designate and appoint my **friend**, **Richard James Carter** of **224 Oak Street, His City, His State**, of as the Guardian of the person and estate of my minor child/ren. In the event that the above-appointed Guardian shall not be able to serve as Guardian for any reason, I designate and appoint my **aunt, Lucy Ellen Smith** of **64 Lake Drive, Her City, Her State**, as the Guardian of the person and estate of my minor child/ren.

Remember to make a first and second choice and to type the complete name of each choice.

C6 Signing Your Will

This is very important in completing your LawPak Last Will and Testament.

◆ Date your will on the line provided.

◆ You must sign your name exactly the same way you typed it on the first page.

◆ Sign your will in ink only in the presence of two (or three, if required) witnesses who are not named in your will. (There is no maximum limit to the number of witnesses.)

◆ If you cannot write, you can put an "X". However, the "X" still must be witnessed.

Examples:

I, **Joseph Allen Jones**, now domiciled in **Your County, Your State**, do make, publish and declare this to be my Last Will and Testament, hereby revoking any and all prior Wills and Codicils heretofore made by me.

I, **Mary nmn Doe**, now domiciled in **Your County, Your State**, do make, publish and declare this to be my Last Will and Testament, hereby revoking any and all prior Wills and Codicils heretofore made by me.

I, **Joseph Allen Jones aka Allen Jones**, now domiciled in **Your County, Your State**, do make, publish and declare this to be my Last Will and Testament, hereby revoking any and all prior Wills and Codicils heretofore made by me.

IN WITNESS WHEREOF, I have signed this Last Will and Testament, consisting of three pages, this page included, on this **19th** day of **February**, **1998**.

_____
signature
Joseph Allen Jones

IN WITNESS WHEREOF, I have signed this Last Will and Testament, consisting of three pages, this page included, on this **1st** day of **September**, **1997**.

_____
signature
Mary nmn Doe

IN WITNESS WHEREOF, I have signed this Last Will and Testament, consisting of three pages, this page included, on this **1st** day of **September**, **1997**.

_____
signature
Joseph Allen Jones
AKA Allen Jones

This is called the execution or the acknowledgment of the will. You are not legally required to initial each page in the lower right corner, but this is added protection against the possibility that someone might remove or replace a page.

C7 Witnesses

There must be at least two witnesses (see state listing below). Lines are provided on which your witnesses must sign and write their address. None of the witnesses may be named in your will or have an interest in your property. In addition, all the witnesses must:

◆ Be legally sane.

◆ Sign their full names and addresses in ink.

◆ Be present to witness your signature.

Remember, your witnesses do not have to read your will; they must only witness your *signature*. You should tell your witnesses this is your Last Will and Testament and that your are signing this document of your own free will.

Example:

We, _____, _____, and _____, the witnesses, sign our names to this instrument, being first duly sworn and do hereby declare to the undersigned authority that the testator signs and executes this instrument as his Last Will and Testament and that he signs it willingly, and that each of us, in the presence and hearing of the testator and in the presence of the other subscribing witnesses, hereby signs this Last Will and Testament as witnesses to the testator's signing, and that to the best of our knowledge the testator is eighteen (18) years of age or older, of sound mind, and under no constraint or undue influence.

(witness signatures)   (witness address, city and state)

_____ residing at _____

States Which Require the Presence of at Least Two Witnesses

Alabama	Illinois	Montana	Pennsylvania
Alaska	Indiana	Nebraska	Rhode Island
Arizona	Iowa	Nevada	South Dakota
Arkansas	Kansas	New Jersey	Tennessee
California	Kentucky	New Mexico	Texas
Colorado	Louisiana	New York	Utah
Connecticut	Maryland	North Carolina	Virginia
Delaware	Michigan	North Dakota	Washington
Florida	Minnesota	Ohio	West Virginia
Georgia	Mississippi	Oklahoma	Wisconsin
Hawaii	Missouri	Oregon	Wyoming
Idaho			

States Which Require the Presence of at Least Three Witnesses

Maine	New Hampshire	South Carolina	Vermont
Massachusetts			

C8 Notary Public

It is not required (except in Louisiana) that your Last Will and Testament be signed and witnessed by a Notary Public to be legal and valid. However, the signature (affidavit) of a notary can be used to self-prove the will in the event all or some of your witnesses are unavailable at the time the will is probated.

If you have your Last Will and Testament notarized, you must sign — and the witnesses should sign their names to the will — in the presence of the Notary Public.

STATE OF _____**Your State**_____)

) SS:

COUNTY OF _____**Your County**_____)

Subscribed, sworn to and acknowledged before me by <u>Your Name</u>, the testator, and subscribed and sworn to before me by <u>Witness' Name</u>, <u>Witness' Name</u>, and <u>Witness' Name</u>, witnesses, who proved to me, with satisfactory evidence, to be the person whose name is subscribed to this instrument and acknowledged signing the foregoing Last Will and Testament and the same is the above's free act and deed.

IN TESTIMONY WHEREOF, I have hereunto subscribed my name and affixed my Notarial Seal at **Your City, Your State** this **25th** day of **November**, **1998**.

_____
signature of Notary Public

_____
signature of Notary Public

C9 What Should I Do With My Will When It is Completed

Once you have signed and dated your LawPak Last Will and Testament in the presence of your witnesses, you must put it in a safe place. Be sure to tell your executor/trix or someone else you trust where you have placed your Last Will and Testament. Otherwise, after your death, no one will know if you have a will or where to find it.

You should review your will periodically to make sure it conforms to your current wishes as to how your estate is to be distributed.

◆ You can put your will in your safety deposit box or leave it with someone you trust. If you put it in your safety deposit box, make sure your executor/trix has a key to the box so he or she can get your will after your death.

◆ You can record it at the courthouse in the county where you live if this service is available. (Not all counties provide this service; for information, check with your county Clerk of Courts.)

Chapter D
Making and Typing the Complete Will Yourself

D1 General Information

If, for whatever reason (additional beneficiaries, additional specific gifts, state requirements, etc.), our fill-in-the-blank forms do not fit your needs, you can type your entire Last Will and Testament yourself using the provisions in this section. (Also see the sample will on page 87. Be sure you first make *a rough draft on paper* so you can correct errors and make changes. Don't forget that your final draft cannot contain any handwritten corrections (only typing machine corrections); nor can any information in the will be crossed out or erased. Once the final draft is complete, destroy all previous drafts to avoid confusion as to what is your original will.

Mandatory

Provisions labeled mandatory should be used in your Will to make it valid and complete.

Optional

Provisions labeled optional may be selected depending on your circumstances and needs.

To prepare your will using the information in this chapter, complete these steps:

1. Read through the chapter and select those provisions which are appropriate for you.

2. Number sequentially each provision (clause) that you have selected, beginning the number one (1). This number will identify the provision in your will.

3. Provide all the necessary information (relationship, name, address, etc.) within each provision.

4. Type your will, selecting in sequence the mandatory and optional provisions which you have numbered.

5. Sign and date your will in the presence of at least two (or three, if required) witnesses.

D2 Mandatory and Optional Provisions

The following are the mandatory and optional provisions you can use to type your Last Will and Testament. You should maintain the same language within the provision as much as possible, replacing the highlighted general information with your personal information.

a Name, Residency, and Revoking Previous Wills   Mandatory ☐

I, **Your Name**, now domiciled of **Your County**, State of **Your State**, being now of sound mind, memory and understanding, do make, publish, and declare this to be my Last Will and Testament, hereby revoking and making null and void any and all prior Last Wills and Testaments and Codicils heretofore made by me. All references herein to this Will shall be construed as referring to this Will only.

b Debt   Mandatory ☐

FIRST: I hereby direct that all my just debts and obligations, including my funeral expenses and the cost of the administration of my estate, be paid as soon after my death as practical, excepting any mortgage indebtedness or other long-term contractual indebtedness secured either by real or personal property or both which may exist as a part of this my estate and may be continued and assumed by the beneficiary of said property. My Executor/trix, with the proper discretion, may pay from my domiciliary estate all or any portion of the cost of ancillary administration and similar proceeding in other jurisdictions.

I direct that my Executor/trix pay out of my estate all inheritance, estate, succession, and other taxes by whatever name called (together with any penalty thereon), assessed by reason of my death with regard to all properties and assets subject to such taxes, whether or not such taxes would be payable by any other recipient or beneficiary or possessor of such property in the absence of this provision. Contribution or reimbursement on account of any such taxes shall not be collected from any such beneficiary or possessor provided that my estate is sufficient to pay such taxes.

c Disinheritance   Optional ☐

If you plan to leave nothing (not even a dollar) to one of your (adult) children, you must specifically disinherit that child or risk having your will challenged. Remember, if you are still legally married, you *cannot* disinherit your spouse.

#☐ I specifically direct that my **relationship**, **person's name**, be disinherited and receive nothing from my estate.

(Repeat the provision as needed.)

Example:

SECOND: I specifically direct that my **son**, **John H. Nogood**, be disinherited and receive nothing from my estate.

^d Specific Gifts of Personal Property   Optional ☐

This provision can be used to make (one or more) specific gifts of personal property (anything but cash gifts or real estate) to anyone and/or any organization you choose. You should also choose an alternate beneficiary of the gift(s).

☐ I give, devise, and bequeath of this my estate, to each of the below-named beneficiaries, specific gifts or personal property, as follows:

a) I give **precise description of item(s)** to my **relationship**, **beneficiary's full name** of **beneficiary's address**, or if (she) (he) (it) fails to survive me by thirty (30) days, to my **relationship**, **alternate beneficiary's name** of **alternate beneficiary's address**.

(Repeat provision as needed for each beneficiary and gift.)

Example:

THIRD: I give, devise, and bequeath of this my estate, to each of the below-named beneficiaries, specific gifts of personal property, as follows:

a) I give **my father's gold pocket watch which has been in my family for three generations and 1000 shares of XYZ Company common stock** to my **son, Edward Arnold Jones** of **2007 Second Street, His City, His State**, or if he fails to survive me by thirty (30) days, to my **son, Matthew Adam Jones** of **6161 Maple Avenue, His City, His State**.

b) I give my **1958 Ford T-bird Serial Number 0344583 and 1000 shares of ABC Company common stock** to my **son, Matthew Adam Jones** of **6161 Maple Avenue, His City, His State**, of if he fails to survive me by thirty (30) days, to my **son, Edward Arnold Jones** of **2007 Second Street, His City, His State**.

c) I give my **complete coin collection and stamp collection** to my **friend, Andrew Michael Harris** of **4200 Oak Avenue, His City, His State**, or if he fails to survive me by thirty (30) days, to my **daughter, Mary Ann Jones** of **33 Maple Avenue, Her City, Her State**.

e Specific Cash Gifts

Optional ☐

This provision will allow you to make (one or more) specific cash gifts to anyone and/or any organization you choose. You should also choose an alternate beneficiary of the cash gift(s).

#☐ I give, devise and bequeath of this my estate, to the below-named beneficiaries specific cash gifts, as follows:

a) I give **written amount of cash in words** Dollars ($**amount in numbers**), to my **relationship**, **beneficiary's full name** of **beneficiary's full address**, or if (she) (he) (it) fails to survive me by thirty (30) days, to my **relationship**, **alternate beneficiary's full name** of **alternate beneficiary's full address**.

(Repeat provision as many times as needed for each beneficiary and cash gift.)

Example:

FOURTH: I give, devise and bequeath of this my estate, to the below-named beneficiaries, specific cash gifts, as follows:

a) I give **Five Thousand and zero cents** Dollars ($**5,000.00**) to my **college**, **The University for All** of **300 Education Avenue, Their City, Their State**, or if it fails to survive me by thirty (30) days to my **brother**, **Earl James Jones** of **10 Sunshine Blvd., His City, His State**.

b) I give **One Thousand and zero cents** Dollars ($**1,000.00**) to **each of my children, in equal shares, Matthew Adam Jones, Mary Ann Jones, and Edward Arnold Jones**, or if they fail to survive me by thirty (30) days to my **wife**, **Cynthia Davis Jones** of **33 Maple Avenue, Her City, Her State**.

c) I give **Two Thousand and zero cents** Dollars ($**2,000.00**) to my **church**, **The Church for All** of **2301 High Street, Its City, Its State**, or if it fails to survive me by thirty (30) days to my **wife**, **Cynthia Davis Jones** of **33 Maple Avenue, Her City, Her State**.

f Specific Gifts of Real Property

Optional ☐

This provision will allow you to leave each parcel of real estate (buildings, land, condominiums, home, etc.) that you own outright to a specific person or organization.

*Note: This provision **should not** be used for any real property that you plan to leave to your principal beneficiary as part of your residuary estate (everything left after your specific gifts).*

☐ I give, devise, bequeath of this my estate, to each of the below-named beneficiaries, specific gifts of real property, as follows:

a) I give the real property commonly known as **precise description of property which may be taken from the deed, if possible** to my **relationship, beneficiary's full name** of **beneficiary's full address**, or s/he (it) fails to survive me by thirty (30) days, to my **relationship, alternate beneficiary's full name** of **alternate beneficiary's full address**.

Example:

☐ I give, devise, bequeath of this my estate, to each of the below-named beneficiaries, specific gifts of real property, as follows:

a) I give the real property commonly known as **Lot 641, Mountain View Resorts, according to the records in the office of the Lake County Recorder, State of Kentucky**, to my **son, Matthew Adam Jones**, of **6161 Maple Avenue, His City, His State**, or s/he (it) fails to survive me by thirty (30) days, to my **wife, Cynthia Davis Jones** of **33 Maple Avenue, Her City, Her State**.

(Repeat provision as needed for each parcel of real estate that is a specific gift.)

g Residuary Clause   **Mandatory** ☐

The residue of your estate is all that remains after your specific cash gifts, specific gifts of personal property and gifts of real estate have been distributed. The person who receives the residue of your estate is called the residuary, or principal, beneficiary.

☐ All the rest, residue and remainder of my estate, whether real, personal, and mixed, of whatever kind and nature, and wheresoever situated, including all property which I may acquire or become entitled to after the execution of this Will, remaining after payment of my debts, funeral expenses, taxes, administration costs and individual bequests, I give, devise and bequeath to my **relationship, principal beneficiary's full name** of **principal beneficiary's full address**.

In the event (she) (he) (it) predeceased me or we both die as the result of a common disaster, then I give, devise, and bequeath the residue of my estate to my **relationship, alternate principal beneficiary's full name** of **alternate principal beneficiary's full address**.

Example:

SIXTH: All the rest, residue and remainder of my estate, whether real, personal, and mixed, of whatever kind and nature, and wheresoever situated, including all property which I may acquire or become entitled to after the execution of this Will, remaining after payment of my debts, funeral expenses, taxes, administration costs and individual bequests, I give, devise and bequeath to my **beloved wife, Cynthia Davis Jones** of **33 Maple Avenue, Her City, Her State**. In the event she predeceased me or we both die as the result of a common disaster, then I give, devise, and bequeath the residue of my estate to my **children, in equal shares, Edward Arnold Jones, Mary Ann Jones, and Matthew Adam Jones**.

Should any such beneficiary named in Article (#) predecease me, then his or her share shall pass per stirpes, in equals shares, that is: (a) if that beneficiary has living issue, the portion of my estate otherwise reserved for that beneficiary shall be distributed among said living issue by right of representation; or (b) if that beneficiary has no living issue, the portion of my estate otherwise reserved for that beneficiary shall be distributed among those of my beneficiaries who did survive me by right of representation.

h Survivorship Period Provision   **Mandatory** ☐

The purpose of this survivorship clause is to prevent the possibility of your property being involved in two different probate actions at the same time, namely your property and the beneficiary receiving the property, if the beneficiary should die soon after you do. The survivorship clause requires that a beneficiary survive you by a specified time. The amount of time can be any number of days but we recommend a 30-day period.

☐ In the event that any person or organization named in this Last Will and Testament shall fail to survive my death by **written number** (**number**) days, it shall be presumed that they failed to survive me.

Example:

SEVENTH: In the event that any person or organization named in the Last Will and Testament shall fail to survive my death by **thirty (30)** days, it shall be presumed that they failed to survive me.

ⓘ Executor/trix Provision Mandatory ☐

The purpose of this provision is to appoint the person who will administer your estate after your death, also appoint at least one alternate Executor/trix.

Note: An Executor is a male administrator; an Executrix is a female administrator.

☐ I appoint my **relationship**, **full name** of **full address** to be Executor/trix of this my Last Will and Testament, to serve without bond. If (she) (he) shall predecease me or, for any reason, fail to serve as Executor/trix, then, in such event, I appoint my **relationship**, **full name** of **full address** to serve as Executor/trix without bond.

Example:

EIGHTH: I appoint my **beloved wife**, **Cynthia Davis Jones** of **33 Maple Avenue, Her City, Her State**, to be the Executrix of this my Last Will and Testament, to serve without bond. If she shall predecease me or, for any reason, fail to serve as Executrix, then, in such event, I appoint my **brother**, **Earl James Jones** of **10 Sun-shine Blvd., His City, His State**, to serve as Executor without bond.

The Executor/trix Provision must contain a clause defining Executor/trix Powers. This clause is mandatory.

Example:

I vest my Executor/trix with full power and discretion, without any court order or proceeding, to sell, pursuant to option and otherwise public or private sale and upon such items as s/he should deem best, any real or personal property belonging to my estate without regard to the necessity of such sale for purpose of paying debts, taxes, or legacies or to retain any such property not so required, without liability for any depreciation thereof; to adjust, compromise, and settle all matters of business and claims in favor of or against my estate; and to do any and all things necessary or proper to complete the administration of my estate, all as fully as I could do if living.

ⓙ Guardianship Provision Optional ☐

If you have minor children, this clause *is mandatory*.

☐ I designate and appoint my **relationship**, **full name** of **full address**, as the Guardian of the person and property of my minor child/ren. In the event that the above-appointed Guardian shall not be able to serve as Guardian, for any reason, I designate my **relationship**, **full name** of **full address**, as the Guardian of the person and property of my minor child/ren.

Example:

NINTH: I designate and appoint my **wife**, **Cynthia Davis Jones** of **33 Maple Avenue, Her City, Her State** as the guardian of the person and property of my minor child/ren. In the event that the above appointed guardian shall not be able to serve as guardian, for any reason, I designate my **brother**, **Earl James Jones** of **10 Sunshine Blvd., His City, His State**., as the guardian of the person and property of my minor child/ren.

It is mandatory that your Guardianship Provision contain a clause stating Guardianship Powers.

a) To the extent permitted by law, I direct that no such person named as guardian in the Last Will and Testament be required to fill a bond or other security of the faithful performance of his/her duties as Guardian of the estate of my minor child/ren.

b) It is my desire that the loving care and treatment of my minor child/ren be trusted to the person designated by me as Guardian of my minor child/ren. I desire the above-named guardian to exercise reasonable and broad discretion in dealing both with the person and property of my minor child/ren so as to be able to do everything deemed advisable in the best interest of my minor child/ren, including performing all acts, taking all proceedings and exercising all such rights and privileges with relation to any matter affecting both the person and property of my minor child/ren, although not specifically mentioned in this Will.

k Signature Provision   Mandatory ☐

Remember, *do not* sign or date your Last and Testament until you are in the presence of your witnesses. (This provision is not numbered.)

Example:

IN WITNESS WHEREOF, I have signed this Last Will and Testament, consisting of three pages, this page included, on this 22nd day of December, 1997.

Your signature
_____

l Witness Provision   Mandatory ☐

You must have at least two witnesses (or three, if required; see Section C7) who acknowledge that you signed your will in their presence. A witness signature and address are both required. (This provision is not numbered.)

Example:

We hereby certify that in our presence, on this date, the above appeared and signed the foregoing instrument and acknowledged it to be (his) (her) Last Will and Testament, and that at the request of and in the presence of the above and in the presence of each other, we have signed our names below as witnesses, and we believe the above to be of sound mind and memory, legally empowered to make a Will, and under no constraint or undue influence.

1. _____   _____
   witness signature   witness address
2. _____   _____
   witness signature   witness signature
3. _____   _____
   witness signature   witness signature

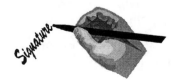

D3 Other Optional Clauses

The following are additional **optional clauses** which can be inserted into your will. We have put these provisions in a separate section because they are rarely used except by a few people.

a Disinheriting a Former Spouse

If, for whatever reason, you want to specifically disinherit a former spouse (someone from whom you are legally divorced), you can insert the following provision:

> # ❑ I have purposely omitted and failed to make any provision, in this my Will, for the benefit of my former spouse, **full name**, as I no longer have any obligation, legally or morally, to provide for (her) (him).

b Canceling Money Owed

If you would like to release your children or anyone else from a debt that they may owe you at the time of your death, the following provision can be inserted:

> # ❑ I hereby release and forgive my **relationship(s)**, **full name(s)**, from any debt or money owed to me, including interest accrued, as of the date of my death. (They) (He) (She) shall not be charged with or required to pay any money advanced or loaned to (them) (him) (her), and I request that all such loans and advances shall be canceled and released.

c No Contest Clause

This provision is used to discourage any of your beneficiaries from challenging your will. Normally, courts will enforce this clause.

> # ❑ In the event that any beneficiary under this Will shall institute in any manner, directly or indirectly, an action against this Will or its provision, or be a party to any litigation involving the validity of this Will, I direct that any property or shared interest given to the contesting beneficiary under this Will be revoked, terminated and void. I further direct that the bequest to the contesting beneficiary shall be considered as part of my residuary estate.

d Burial Instructions

If you want to insert this clause, make sure that the executor of your will is aware of your burial request and has a copy of your will to support the request. The clause is worded as follows:

> # ❑ I hereby direct that upon my death, my Executor/trix contact **name of funeral home or individual** where I have paid for funeral arrangements and burial at **place of burial**.

Or:

> # ❑ I hereby direct that upon my death, my body be cremated and my ashes shall be **your decision**.

e Pets

You can provide for your pets in your will by leaving money to a friend with instructions on providing care.

❑ I direct that my **description of pet**, **pet's name**, be well cared for, and direct that **your instructions for providing care and/or money**.

f Savings Provision

The savings clause is protection against your will being nullified by a court which voids one or more provisions in the will. This possibility is very remote, but you should type this provision into your will as protection against any remote possibilities.

❑ In the event any part, clause, provision or condition of this Will should be held invalid, void, or inoperative, I direct that such invalidity shall not affect any other part, clause, provision or condition hereof this my Last Will and Testament. It is my intention that each of the separate provisions shall be independent of each of the others and that the remainder of this Will shall be strictly enforced as though such part, clause, provision or condition had not been contained herein.

Provisions to Avoid

◆ Avoid unusual or weird provisions. Do not require a beneficiary to perform certain acts. The Court will probably declare it void.

◆ Avoid restrictions on the use of property, particularly if it is against public policy.

◆ Avoid restrictions regarding marriage of a beneficiary.

Chapter E
The Probate Process

E1 Introduction

Probate is the legal (court-supervised) process created to maintain order and direct the distribution of property, collection of assets, payment of bills, and payment of taxes on a person's death. Usually, it takes at least six to eighteen months to probate an uncontested estate. The three primary reasons for probate are:

♦ to protect your property so that the property is not given out on a first-come basis, but as you have requested in your will.

♦ to settle title (change of ownership) so that property can be formally transferred to the correct living individuals or organizations.

♦ to settle all debts and claims against the estate.

E2 The Steps in the Probate Process

1 Find the Will

The first step is to determine if there is a will and where it is located. It is most often in the deceased's personal papers or safe deposit box. It is a crime to conceal or destroy a will, and the will must be submitted to Probate Court within a certain time period (normally 30 days) after the person's death.

2 Submit the Will to Probate

The original will is sent to the Probate Court in the district where the deceased had their permanent residence at the time of death. The executor requests (petitions) the Probate Court to approve the will as the Last Will and Testament of the deceased. If there is no will, the Petition for Probate requests the judge to declare that the deceased died intestate and that his or her property be distributed in accordance with the state intestacy laws. Petitions for the probate of a will are simple forms, which are available at the Probate Court.

3 Notice to Heirs/Beneficiaries

After the petition is filed with the Probate Court, the court will normally order that notice of the probate petition be given to the heirs/beneficiaries and other interested parties who may be named in the will. Notice in most states means that a legal notice (publication) must be placed in the local newspaper and written notice with a copy of the Petition of Probate and your will be sent to each of your beneficiaries and heirs. This is the time for anyone who wishes to contest the will to make it known to the Probate Court. Publication is normally a requirement of probate which most individuals dislike because all records are made public.

4 Appointment of the Executor

Approximately six weeks after the Petition for Probate is filed and three weeks after publication, the probate judge has a hearing. If no one contests the will, the court will appoint the executor, usually the person named in the will, and admit the will into probate (declare the will to be valid). Once appointed by the court, the executor will take legal title of the deceased's property (authorized by letters of testamentary signed by the probate judge), prepare and file an estate inventory of all the deceased's property, assets, and debts.

5 Filing the Inventory

The estate inventory is submitted to the court (within one to three months depending upon state law) and becomes a matter of public record. Nonprobate property (jointly held property, life insurance or retirement benefits payable to a named beneficiary, or assets in a living trust) will not be included in the probate estate inventory.

6 Payment of Creditors

The executor has an obligation to notify all known creditors within a reasonable time period so that they may file a claim for payment.

7 Payment of Debts, Fees, Expenses, and Taxes

The Executor will determine the remaining debts (legal fees, utility bills, etc.) and make payment since these debts will influence the amount of federal and state estate taxes due on the estate, if any.

8 Filing Estate Tax Returns

It is the responsibility of the Executor to prepare, or have a professional (lawyer or accountant) prepare, the deceased's federal and state estate tax returns, which will include the property in the estate, reduced by the amount of claims and deductions. If an estate is worth less than $650,000.00 in 1999 (value of all property in the estate), no federal tax is due since this is the allowable tax-free amount. Until the tax returns are accepted and the final tax liability is paid (if any is due), the Executor should not distribute all the assets of the estate. The percentage of state estate taxes due will vary by state law. In many states, a return must still be filed even if there are no taxes due. The Executor should always wait for a final notice from the government that no further taxes are due.

9 Distribution of Inheritance to Beneficiaries

After all the creditors have been paid and all inheritance taxes are paid, the Executor will file a Petition for Distribution to pay the remaining property to the beneficiaries or heirs of the estate. The Executor can only distribute the remaining property according to the terms of the deceased's will after all taxes, claims, bills, and expenses are paid, or the amounts are set aside and there is written court approval. Before any property is transferred to the beneficiaries, a release form is prepared and signed by each indicating that they accept the distribution in full settlement of any claims. The beneficiaries may also receive a copy of the final account (detailed financial report) of the estate, which is filed with the Probate Court.

10 Closing the Estate

The executor will submit the final account and releases from the beneficiaries to the Probate Court and request that the final account be allowed. When the court has accepted (allowed) the final account as a complete and accurate record of the settlement of the estate, the estate will be closed and the executor will be discharged of his duties and liabilities.

E3 Advantages and Disadvantages of Probate

Probate has these primary advantages:

- ◆ Probate is a court-supervised process which protects your property while it is being distributed to your beneficiaries or heirs.
- ◆ Probate formally transfers or clears title to property from your name into the names of your beneficiaries or heirs.
- ◆ Probate allows a limited time period for creditors to make claims against the estate.

There are a few disadvantages to Probate:

- **Cost**. The probate process involves some costs, primarily the fees paid to the executor and to the probate attorney. These fees are regulated and will vary by state law. Most states have laws which set the fees based on a certain percentage of the net or gross worth of the probated estate. Other states set minimum fees; others require the attorney and executor to offer proof of time spent to justify their fees. Depending on such fee variations, the total worth of the estate, and the costs of publication and appraisals, probating a typical estate will cost approximately five to ten percent of the total worth of the estate.

- **Delays**. Many delays are built into the probate process: the number of weeks required for publication, the required period during which creditors can make claims against the estate, filing the tax return at least nine months after death. Other delays may be caused by the number of cases before the probate court and the numerous tasks to be accomplished to settle the estate. On average, it will take at least six to eighteen months to completely probate an estate.

- **Public Notice**. The probate process requires public notice of the death. As discussed, notice of death through a publication must be given to the public, and all heirs and beneficiaries must be given specific notice and a copy of the will. Also, the will and all court papers related to the estate of the deceased are public records; this means anyone — even strangers or disinherited individuals — can review them any time after these documents become public record.

E4 Estate Taxes

Federal and state tax laws change constantly. Please be aware that information contained in this book is correct at the time of writing; if you have specific questions about estate taxes, seek the advice of professional tax planners.

a Federal Taxes

Much has been written about avoiding probate, primarily to avoid estate taxes. But for all practical purposes, only a small percentage of people pay federal estate taxes. This is because there are two separate exemptions or deductions from federal estate tax:

◆ First, there is the marital deduction for property you leave your spouse. Any property you leave to your spouse at your death is entirely tax-free from federal taxes (and usually from state tax); there is no dollar limit.

◆ Second, there is exemption of $650,000.00 (based on the total worth of the estate, not the amount to be distributed to any one recipient) which affects property you leave to anyone (person or organization) other than your spouse. This means that if your estate is worth $650,000.00 or less, the estate will not pay federal estate taxes, no matter who you leave it to, based on current law.

Note: An estate tax problem can occur if your spouse dies with a total estate worth more than $650,000.00 (his/her estate plus yours). If his or her estate does exceed the $650,000.00 maximum limit, his or her estate will pay federal taxes unless additional tax planning methods are utilized to avoid the estate taxes before your spouse's death.

Note: The federal tax is based on your estate, which includes all property in your name alone, but does not include your spouse's half of the community property.

There are some tax revisions you should be aware of. In 1997, Congress passed new federal tax laws (Taxpayer Relief Act), which give individuals an increase in the amount of assets that are exempt from federal taxes to the heirs of an estate. The federal taxes owed on an estate can be as high as sixty percent on any amounts above the amounts stated below.

Year	Amount	Year	Amount
1998	$625,000.00	2004	$850,000.00
1999	$650,000.00	2005	$950,000.00
2000-2001	$675,000.00	2006 and after	$1 million
2002-2003	$700,000.00		

NOTE: For owners of farms and small businesses, the tax exemptions are substantial. The new law increases the Unified Credit, or the amount that you can leave to heirs before federal taxes are imposed, to $1.3 million from $600,000.00 for certain family-owned businesses. The exclusion only takes effect when the person who died owned a set percentage of the company and the company accounted for a large share (at least fifty percent) of the deceased person's assets. In addition, the heirs have to be actively involved in the business for a set number of years before and after the benefactor's death.

Under the unlimited marital deduction, your spouse may avoid estate taxes if you leave everything to him or her in your will and s/he is a U.S. citizen. An annual tax return must be filed for income that you earned up to the date of your death. The return must be filed with the Internal Revenue Service by April 15 of the following year. Your surviving spouse may file a joint tax return for the year of your death and pay under a joint filer's tax rate. On the line where the tax return is signed, the spouse must indicate in writing that he or she is filing as a surviving spouse.

b State Taxes

Although your estate may not have to pay federal estate taxes, the estate may still be subject to state inheritance taxes. State inheritance laws vary by state. In some states, tax rates may vary depending on the relationship of the beneficiary to the deceased. Some states provide for deductions and exemptions in tax computations, while others do not. A number of states do not have any inheritance taxes (California, for example); other states exempt all property transferred to a surviving spouse (New York). If your state is subject to inheritance taxes, the percentage is normally small. Check with your state's taxing authorities to determine the exact percentages or exemptions.

Chapter F
Organizing Your Estate

The task of arranging the deceased's financial matters is the responsibility of the remaining family members. It is very important that family members be provided with a list of your financial documents and their location so they may close your estate. Also, your survivors should have a clear understanding, from written documents, of all professional fees to be charged by attorneys or accountants and of funeral expenses before any work is begun to settle the estate.

F1 Checklist for Immediate Action

Here is a checklist of things your survivors will have to do following your death. It will help you determine what financial items should be maintained with your estate papers to assist your survivors.

◆ Make funeral arrangements. (Establish their fee for services.)

◆ Notify relatives and friends.

◆ Collect copies of the following:

- Last Will and Testament
- Certified copies of death certificates
- Insurance policies
- Latest financial statement
- Bank statements, account numbers and location
- Birth certificate
- Marriage license
- Social Security information
  Obtain the Social Security number of the deceased. Apply to nearest Social Security Office in person and bring Social Security number of deceased, certified copy of death certificate, and proof of relationship: marriage license and birth certificate.
- Veterans Affairs number and records
  Inquire in person at the local Office of Veterans Affairs. Deliver required documentation such as birth certificate, Social Security number, death certificate, and veteran's records.
- List of employer benefits
  Contact the deceased's employer benefits department immediately and request a listing of death benefits payable; determine how the benefits are paid. Provide employee benefits department a certified death certificate and other documentation required.
- Tax Returns (last three years)
  Contact attorney to notify witnesses to Last Will and Testament and schedule a meeting for settling the estate and filing tax returns, etc. (Establish the attorney's fee for services.)

◆ Advise the Executor of the estate.
  The Executor should adjust ownership of any insurance policies owned by the deceased, retitle real estate and automobiles that were owned by the deceased, and inventory the contents of the deceased's safety deposit box and the entire estate with an attorney.

◆ Contact banks to verify status of accounts (checking and savings) and safety deposit box.

◆ Notify insurance brokers so they can modify homeowners or auto casualty insurance. Obtain death claim form and return it to the insurance company with a certified copy of the death certificate and policy.

◆ Locate securities and contact broker to retitle securities.

◆ Contact accountant to prepare all necessary tax returns to close the estate. (Establish fee for accountant's services.)

F2 Financial Power of Attorney

One of the most neglected documents that everyone should draft is a Durable Power of Attorney. This legal document enables you to appoint and authorize an individual (attorney-in-fact) to make financial management decisions on your behalf and manage your affairs should you become incapacitated or legally incompetent. LawPak has a publication which provides step-by-step instructions and forms on drafting and executing a legal Durable Power of Attorney. (See order form in the back of this publication.) A Power of Attorney agreement should not be placed in a safe deposit box as that would leave this document inaccessible at the time it may be needed. You should execute two copies and deliver one to the person holding the power (attorney-in-fact); keep the other copy in a safe place.

F3 Living Will

A Living Will is a legal document that allows you to define your wishes, for family and physicians, concerning your medical treatment in advance of becoming incapacitated. It allows you to express in writing your position on being kept alive indefinitely and provides instructions about life support and resuscitation efforts. LawPak has a publication with step-by-step instructions and forms for drafting a legal Living Will. (See order form in the back of this publication.) A Living Will should not be placed in a safe deposit box, but in a safe place that is more accessible.

F3 Funeral Arrangements

When a loved one dies is not the best time to make decisions and consider costs. Your family will have little time to think about funeral options and will not be in the best frame of mind to make decisions. Take the time now to consider some choices and discuss your thoughts with your family about the type of ceremony and burial procedures you would prefer.

If you choose to prepay for a funeral, the Federal Trade Commission states that you should consider the following:

◆ Funeral directors are required to itemize prices and provide consumers with price lists and price information over the telephone so the consumer can compare costs.

◆ Make sure you know what you are paying for:
  - casket or cremation ($300 to $12,000)
  - burial vault
  - funeral services
  - flowers
  - cemetery lot
  - monuments and memorials

◆ What happens to the money that you have prepaid? Is it put into an escrow account? Is there interest income from these prepaid amounts?

◆ What is your protection if the funeral company goes out of business?

◆ Can you cancel the contract and receive the full refund of the money you have prepaid?

◆ What if you move to another location? Can the prepaid funeral be transferred and what will it cost?

◆ Make sure you keep copies of all funeral contracts and prepaid documents. Tell a family member where the documents are located.

F4 Letter of Instruction

You may create detailed written instructions concerning your funeral arrangements which family members may then use as a reference to implement your preferences. Death is inevitable. You can work through the details now or leave the burden to grieving family members.

◆ Determine:
- what you would like done with your body (burial, cemetery and plot, cremation).
- what kind of grave marker you would like.
- what funeral home you prefer.
- what type service you would like.
- what you prefer in the way of flowers, music, and religious readings.

◆ Write your own obituary.

◆ Think of ideas for a eulogy.

◆ Request certain items you want buried with you.

Give a copy of your letter of instructions to a family member and put another copy with your estate papers.

Biographical Information *Husband*

FULL NAME	**NAMES OF CHILDREN**
FIRST MIDDLE LAST	NAME
STREET ADDRESS	
	CITY STATE TELEPHONE
CITY STATE ZIP	NAME
TELEPHONE	
	CITY STATE TELEPHONE
RESIDENT SINCE (Date)	NAME
PLACE OF BIRTH (City, County, State)	
	CITY STATE TELEPHONE
DATE OF BIRTH (Month, Day, Year)	NAME
SOCIAL SECURITY NUMBER	
	CITY STATE TELEPHONE
OCCUPATION	NAME
EMPLOYED BY (OR RETIRED)	
	CITY STATE TELEPHONE
MARITAL STATUS	NAME
NAME OF SPOUSE	
	CITY STATE TELEPHONE
NAME OF FATHER	MILITARY SERVICE BRANCH RANK
FATHER'S PLACE OF BIRTH YEAR	DATE OF ENLISTMENT DATE OF DISCHARGE
MOTHER'S MAIDEN NAME	SERIAL NUMBER
MOTHER'S PLACE OF BIRTH YEAR	RELATIVES AND FRIENDS TO NOTIFY
EDUCATION Elementary	NAME/RELATIONSHIP
High School	CITY STATE TELEPHONE
College	NAME/RELATIONSHIP
RELIGIOUS AFFILIATION	CITY STATE TELEPHONE
FRATERNAL/SERVICE/UNION MEMBERSHIPS	NAME/RELATIONSHIP
FRATERNAL/SERVICE/UNION MEMBERSHIPS	CITY STATE TELEPHONE
SPECIAL RECOGNITIONS	NAME/RELATIONSHIP
SPECIAL RECOGNITIONS	CITY STATE TELEPHONE

Funeral Arrangements   Husband

FUNERAL HOME TO CONTACT
_____

ADDRESS OF FUNERAL HOME
_____

TELEPHONE
_____

NAME OF FUNERAL DIRECTOR
_____

LOCATION OF PRE-ARRANGEMENT CONTRACT
_____

LOCATION(S) PREFERRED FOR SERVICES
_____
_____
_____

RELIGIOUS SERVICES
_____

OFFICIATING CLERGYMAN
_____

MILITARY SERVICES
_____

FRATERNAL SERVICES
_____

CONTACT PERSON _____ TELEPHONE

PALLBEARERS _____ HONORARY PALLBEARERS
_____
_____
_____
_____
_____

MUSIC   FLOWERS
_____ _____
_____ _____

MEMORIALS
_____
_____

OTHER REQUESTS
_____
_____
_____

CEMETERY ARRANGEMENTS
_____

NAME OF CEMETERY
_____

ADDRESS
_____

CITY _____ STATE

LOCATION OF DEED
_____

PLOT IN NAME OF
_____

SECTION _____ PLOT NUMBER _____ BLOCK

SPECIAL INSTRUCTIONS
_____
_____
_____
_____

Biographical Information Wife

FULL NAME

_____
FIRST   MIDDLE   LAST

STREET ADDRESS
_____

CITY   STATE   ZIP
_____

TELEPHONE
_____

RESIDENT SINCE (Date)
_____

PLACE OF BIRTH (City, County, State)
_____

DATE OF BIRTH (Month, Day, Year)
_____

SOCIAL SECURITY NUMBER
_____

OCCUPATION
_____

EMPLOYED BY (OR RETIRED)
_____

MARITAL STATUS
_____

NAME OF SPOUSE
_____

NAME OF FATHER
_____

FATHER'S PLACE OF BIRTH   YEAR
_____

MOTHER'S MAIDEN NAME
_____

MOTHER'S PLACE OF BIRTH   YEAR
_____

EDUCATION   Elementary
_____

               High School
_____

               College
_____

RELIGIOUS AFFILIATION
_____

FRATERNAL/SERVICE/UNION MEMBERSHIPS
_____

FRATERNAL/SERVICE/UNION MEMBERSHIPS
_____

SPECIAL RECOGNITIONS
_____

SPECIAL RECOGNITIONS
_____

NAMES OF CHILDREN

NAME
_____

CITY   STATE   TELEPHONE
_____

NAME
_____

CITY   STATE   TELEPHONE
_____

NAME
_____

CITY   STATE   TELEPHONE
_____

NAME
_____

CITY   STATE   TELEPHONE
_____

NAME
_____

CITY   STATE   TELEPHONE
_____

NAME
_____

CITY   STATE   TELEPHONE
_____

MILITARY SERVICE   BRANCH   RANK
_____

DATE OF ENLISTMENT   DATE OF DISCHARGE
_____

SERIAL NUMBER
_____

RELATIVES AND FRIENDS TO NOTIFY

NAME/RELATIONSHIP
_____

CITY   STATE   TELEPHONE
_____

NAME/RELATIONSHIP
_____

CITY   STATE   TELEPHONE
_____

NAME/RELATIONSHIP
_____

CITY   STATE   TELEPHONE
_____

NAME/RELATIONSHIP
_____

CITY   STATE   TELEPHONE
_____

Funeral Arrangements *Wife*

FUNERAL HOME TO CONTACT _____

ADDRESS OF FUNERAL HOME _____

TELEPHONE _____

NAME OF FUNERAL DIRECTOR _____

LOCATION OF PRE-ARRANGEMENT CONTRACT _____

LOCATION(S) PREFERRED FOR SERVICES _____

_____

_____

RELIGIOUS SERVICES _____

OFFICIATING CLERGYMAN _____

MILITARY SERVICES _____

FRATERNAL SERVICES _____

CONTACT PERSON _____ TELEPHONE _____

PALLBEARERS   HONORARY PALLBEARERS

_____   _____

_____   _____

_____   _____

_____   _____

_____   _____

_____   _____

MUSIC   FLOWERS

_____   _____

_____   _____

MEMORIALS

_____

_____

OTHER REQUESTS

_____

_____

CEMETERY ARRANGEMENTS

NAME OF CEMETERY _____

ADDRESS _____

CITY _____ STATE _____

LOCATION OF DEED _____

PLOT IN NAME OF _____

SECTION _____ PLOT NUMBER _____ BLOCK _____

SPECIAL INSTRUCTIONS

_____

_____

_____

_____

Safe Deposit Box Contents

As a general rule, only those documents and valuables that are irreplaceable or difficult to replace need to be kept in a safe deposit box. Items that can be replaced with minimal inconvenience, such as passports, or those frequently needed for reference, such as canceled checks, can be kept in a safe place at home. If documents are stored at home, it may be a good idea to keep copies in a safe deposit box.

When filling out the rental forms for a safe deposit box, you should be aware that if the renter dies, there are specific rules governing access to the box and its contents. Many people assume that, should they die, a joint box holder or authorized deputy can immediately remove necessary documents from the box. In many states, the safe deposit box is sealed upon the death of the renter. If there is a surviving tenant or deputy, he or she would not have access to the contents of the box until the Inheritance Tax Department of the County Auditor makes an inventory of the box and removes the will for probate.

The arrangements for the tax inventory are usually made by the deceased person's attorney. It generally takes a minimum of two or three days and frequently a month before the process is completed. After the tax inventory, the county auditor issues an authorization stating who may remove contents from the box.

Banks normally do not recommend what a tenant should or should not keep in a safe deposit box. However, anything that would be needed immediately following death, such as wills or insurance policies, probably should not be kept in the safe deposit box.

The original copy of a will can be kept in a fireproof safe or with an attorney. If the original will is kept with an attorney, it is a good idea to keep a copy of the will in the safe deposit box and another copy of the will at home where it is readily accessible for review.

Many box holders keep valuable articles, such as coin or stamp collections, that belong to their children or spouse. These should not be in their safe deposit box since there is a presumption that articles in the box belong to the box holder. If such items are kept in a box, it is important to keep with them any papers denoting the owner and the origin of ownership or purchase.

Items That Should Be in a Safe Deposit Box

- Abstracts of Properties
- Adoption Papers
- Appraisals of Valuables
- Automobiles Titles
- Birth Certificates (original)
- Bonds (U.S. Savings, corporate, government, church)
- Certificates of Deposit
- Citizenship Papers
- Coin and Stamp Collections
- Contracts and Agreements
- Copyrights and Original Text
- Court Decrees
- Credit Card List (with phone #s)
- Death Certificates
- Deeds and Titles
- Disability Insurance (list of amounts, insurers, numbers)
- Divorce Decrees and Agreements
- Employment Contracts
- Household Inventories (for insurance)
- Jewelry (valuable items and family heirlooms)
- Life Insurance (list of amounts, insurers, numbers)
- Major Assets and Savings Accounts (listing)
- Marriage Certificates (original)
- Military Discharge Papers
- Mortgage Instruments and Cancellations
- Negatives of Important Photographs
- Naturalization Papers
- Patents and Original Designs
- Pension Certificates
- Precious Metals
- Promissory Notes
- Property and Casualty Insurance Policies
- Savings Certificates
- Stock or Bond Certificates
- Treasured Photo Negatives
- Trust Agreements (you and attorney should have copies)
- Valued Letters
- Veterans Papers
- Wills (you and attorney should have copies)
- Videotape and Photos of Household Contents

Items That Should Not be in a Safe Deposit Box

- Burial Instructions
- Cemetery Deeds and Requests
- Funeral Arrangements Requests
- Homeowner or Auto Insurance Policies
- Large Amounts of Cash (causes IRS questions)
- Life Insurance Policies (put list only in the box)
- Medical and Disability Policies (put list only in the box)
- Power of Attorney
- Property Owned by Someone Else (will be taxed as yours unless clearly documented as to origin or gift)

Document Location and Records

Name _____ Date _____

Social Security No. _____ - _____ - _____ Spouse's Social Security No. _____ - _____ - _____

A. Residence Locations _____

_____

B. Safe Deposit Box Number _____ Bank _____

  Bank Address _____

C. Office Location _____

D. Other Location _____

Document	A	B	C	D
My Will (original)	[ ]	[ ]	[ ]	[ ]
My Will (copy)	[ ]	[ ]	[ ]	[ ]
Powers of Attorney Agreements	[ ]	[ ]	[ ]	[ ]
Burial Instructions	[ ]	[ ]	[ ]	[ ]
Cemetery Plot Deed	[ ]	[ ]	[ ]	[ ]
Spouse's Will (original)	[ ]	[ ]	[ ]	[ ]
Spouse's Will (copy)	[ ]	[ ]	[ ]	[ ]
Document Appointing Guardians	[ ]	[ ]	[ ]	[ ]
Written special Bequest List	[ ]	[ ]	[ ]	[ ]
Trust Agreements	[ ]	[ ]	[ ]	[ ]
Life Insurance (group)	[ ]	[ ]	[ ]	[ ]
Life Insurance (individual)	[ ]	[ ]	[ ]	[ ]
Other Death Benefits	[ ]	[ ]	[ ]	[ ]
Property & Casualty Insurance	[ ]	[ ]	[ ]	[ ]
Health Insurance Policy	[ ]	[ ]	[ ]	[ ]
Homeowners Insurance Policy	[ ]	[ ]	[ ]	[ ]
List of Residence Contents	[ ]	[ ]	[ ]	[ ]
Car Insurance Policy	[ ]	[ ]	[ ]	[ ]
Employment Contracts	[ ]	[ ]	[ ]	[ ]
Partnership Agreements	[ ]	[ ]	[ ]	[ ]
List of Checking/Savings Accounts	[ ]	[ ]	[ ]	[ ]
Bank Statements & Checks	[ ]	[ ]	[ ]	[ ]
Brokerage Statements	[ ]	[ ]	[ ]	[ ]
Mutual Funds Statements	[ ]	[ ]	[ ]	[ ]
List of Credit Cards	[ ]	[ ]	[ ]	[ ]
Certificates of Deposit	[ ]	[ ]	[ ]	[ ]
Stock and Bond Certificates	[ ]	[ ]	[ ]	[ ]

Document	A	B	C	D
Checkbooks	[ ]	[ ]	[ ]	[ ]
Savings Passbooks	[ ]	[ ]	[ ]	[ ]
List of Investments	[ ]	[ ]	[ ]	[ ]
Safe Combination (business)	[ ]	[ ]	[ ]	[ ]
Safe Combination (home)	[ ]	[ ]	[ ]	[ ]
Stock Purchase Plan	[ ]	[ ]	[ ]	[ ]
Profit Sharing Plan	[ ]	[ ]	[ ]	[ ]
Income and Gift Tax Returns	[ ]	[ ]	[ ]	[ ]
Titles & Deeds to Real Estate	[ ]	[ ]	[ ]	[ ]
Title Insurance	[ ]	[ ]	[ ]	[ ]
Rental Property Records	[ ]	[ ]	[ ]	[ ]
Debt Notes & Loan Agreements	[ ]	[ ]	[ ]	[ ]
List of Stored Possessions	[ ]	[ ]	[ ]	[ ]
List of Loaned Possessions	[ ]	[ ]	[ ]	[ ]
Auto Ownership Records	[ ]	[ ]	[ ]	[ ]
Boat Ownership Records	[ ]	[ ]	[ ]	[ ]
Birth Certificates	[ ]	[ ]	[ ]	[ ]
Citizenship Papers	[ ]	[ ]	[ ]	[ ]
Adoption Papers	[ ]	[ ]	[ ]	[ ]
Military Discharge Papers	[ ]	[ ]	[ ]	[ ]
Marriage Certificate	[ ]	[ ]	[ ]	[ ]
Children's Birth Certificates	[ ]	[ ]	[ ]	[ ]
Divorce/Separation Papers	[ ]	[ ]	[ ]	[ ]
Names & Addresses of Relatives	[ ]	[ ]	[ ]	[ ]
Names & Addresses of Friends	[ ]	[ ]	[ ]	[ ]
Passports	[ ]	[ ]	[ ]	[ ]
Tax Returns	[ ]	[ ]	[ ]	[ ]

Other Personal Records

S = Single, J = Joint

Bank Checking Accounts

Bank _____ Owner (S,J) _____ No. _____

Bank _____ Owner (S,J) _____ No. _____

Bank Savings Accounts

Bank _____ Owner (S,J) _____ No. _____

Bank _____ Owner (S,J) _____ No. _____

Money Market Fund Accounts

Bank _____ Owner (S,J) _____ No. _____

Bank _____ Owner (S,J) _____ No. _____

Mutual Fund Accounts

Bank _____ Owner (S,J) _____ No. _____

Bank _____ Owner (S,J) _____ No. _____

Bank _____ Owner (S,J) _____ No. _____

Bank _____ Owner (S,J) _____ No. _____

Bank _____ Owner (S,J) _____ No. _____

Bank _____ Owner (S,J) _____ No. _____

Bank _____ Owner (S,J) _____ No. _____

Bank _____ Owner (S,J) _____ No. _____

Government Savings Bonds

Series _____ Serial No. _____ No. _____ No. _____

Series _____ Serial No. _____ No. _____ No. _____

Broker Accounts

Broker _____ Owner (S,J) _____ No. _____

Broker _____ Owner (S,J) _____ No. _____

Broker _____ Owner (S,J) _____ No. _____

Securities Held Directly (not at a brokerage firm)

Security _____ Owner (S,J) _____ No. _____

Security _____ Owner (S,J) _____ No. _____

Security _____ Owner (S,J) _____ No. _____

Security _____ Owner (S,J) _____ No. _____

Limited Partnerships

General Partner _____ Owner (C, S, J) _____

Title of Transaction _____

Mailing Address _____

Government Benefits

Military Service Number _____ Branch _____

Service Dates _____ to _____ Percent Disability _____ Amount _____

Retirement Income _____ Commencement Date _____

Civil Service Employment _____

Benefits Retained _____

Loans or Accounts Payable to You

From Whom _____ Amount _____

From Whom _____ Amount _____

Loans Outstanding (non-real estate)

Bank or Other Lender _____ Amount _____

Bank or Other Lender _____ Amount _____

Bank or Other Lender _____ Amount _____

Residence Information

Primary Residence Mortgage Holder _____

Amount of Payments _____ Due Date _____

Additional Mortgage Holder _____

Amount of Payments _____ Due Date _____

Additional Residence Address _____

Amount of Payments _____ Due Date _____

Additional Mortgage Holder _____

Amount of Payments _____ Due Date _____

Fire & Casualty Insurance Contracts

Auto, Company _____ Policy No. _____

Homeowners, Company _____ Policy No. _____

Fire, Company _____ Policy No. _____

Liability, Company _____ Policy No. _____

Theft, Company _____ Policy No. _____

Umbrella Liability, Company _____ Policy No. _____

BLANK FORMS

Last Will and Testament Without Minor Children

Forms are perforated for easy removal. Fold carefully and tear along the perforation to remove pages.

Last Will and Testament

of

John Michael Doe

I, **John Michael Doe** now domiciled of

Your County, State of **Your** ,

being now of sound mind, memory and understanding, do make, publish and declare this to be my **LAST WILL AND TESTAMENT**, hereby revoking and making null and void any and all prior Last Wills and Testaments and Codicils heretofore made by me. All references herein to this Will shall be construed as referring to this Will only.

FIRST: I hereby direct that all my just debts and obligations, including my funeral expenses and the cost of the administration of my estate, be paid as soon after my death as practical, excepting any mortgage indebtedness or other long-term contractual indebtedness secured either by real or personal property, both which may exist as a part of this my estate and may be continued and assumed by the beneficiary of said property. My Executor/trix, with the proper discretion, may pay from my domiciliary estate all or any portion of the cost of ancillary administration and similar proceeding in other jurisdictions.

I direct that my Executor/trix pay out of my estate all inheritance, estate, succession, and other taxes by whatever name called (together with any penalty thereon), assessed by reason of my death with regard to all properties and assets subject to such taxes, whether or not such taxes would be payable by any other recipient or beneficiary or possessor of such property in the absence of this provision. Contribution or reimbursement on account of any such taxes shall not be collected from any such beneficiary or possessor provided that my estate is sufficient to pay such taxes.

SECOND: I give, devise, and bequeath of this my estate, to each of the below-named beneficiaries specific gifts of personal property, as follows:

a) I give **my coin collection and golf clubs**

to my **brother** , **William Lee Doe** of **2000 Main Street, His City, His State** of if s/he (it) fails to survive me by thirty (30) days, to my **sister** , **Pamela Doe Smith** , of **101 Elm Street, Her City, Her State** .

b) I give **my 1940 Ford Serial Number 9876543, 14K gold ring with ruby stone, and pocket watch** to my **nephew** , **Robert Lee Doe** of **2000 Main Street, His City, His State** of if s/he (it) fails to survive me by thirty (30) days, to my **sister** , **Pamela Doe Smith** , of **101 Elm Street, Her City, Her State** .

page **1** of **5** **Your Initials**

WILL WITHOUT MINOR CHILDREN - SAMPLE

THIRD: I give, devise and bequeath of this my estate, to the below-named beneficiaries specific cash gifts, as follows:

a) I give _____ **One Thousand and zero cents** _____ Dollars ($ **1,000**) to my _____ **nephew** _____, **Thomas Andrew Smith** _____, of _____ **101 Elm Street, His City, His State** _____ or if s/he (it) fails to survive me by thirty (30) days, to my _____ **brother** _____, _____ **William Lee Doe** _____ of _____ _____ **2000 Main Street, His City, His State** _____.

b) I give _____ **Two Thousand and Five Hundred and zero cents** _____ Dollars ($ **2,500**) to my _____ **church** _____, **The People's Church** _____, of _____ **88 S. Fourth Street, Its City, Its State** _____ or if s/he (it) fails to survive me by thirty (30) days, to my _____ **wife** _____, _____ **Mary nmn Doe** _____ of _____ _____ **224 Travelers Lane, Her City, Her State** _____.

FOURTH: All the rest and remainder of my estate, whether real, personal, and mixed, or whatever kind of nature, and wheresoever situated, including all property which I may acquire or become entitled to after the execution of this Will, remaining after payment of my debts, funeral expenses, taxes, administration costs and individual bequests, I give, devise and bequeath to my _____ **wife** _____, **Mary nmn Doe** _____ of _____ **224 Travelers Lane, Her City, Her State** _____.

In the event s/he has predeceased me or we both die as the result of a common disaster, then I give, devise and bequeath my estate to my **brother and sister (in equal shares)**, _____ **William Lee Doe and Pamela Doe Smith** _____, of _____ **2000 Main** _____ **Street, His City, His State and 101 Elm Street, Her City, Her State** _____.

Should any such beneficiary named in Article Four predecease me, then his or her share shall pass per stirpes, that is: (a) if that beneficiary has living issue, the portion of my estate otherwise reserved for that beneficiary shall be distributed among said living issue by right of representation; or (b) if that beneficiary has no living issue, the portion of my estate otherwise reserved for that beneficiary shall be distributed among those of my beneficiaries who did survive me by right of representation.

FIFTH: In the event that any person named in this Last Will and Testament shall fail to survive my death by thirty (30) days, it shall be presumed that they failed to survive me.

SIXTH: I appoint my _____ **wife** _____, **Mary nmn Doe** _____, to be the Executor/trix of this my Last Will and Testament, to serve without bond. If s/he shall predecease me or, for any reason, fail to serve to Executor/trix, then in such event, I appoint my _____ **brother** _____, _____ **William Lee Doe** _____ to serve as Executor/trix without bond.

SEVENTH: In the event, any part, clause, provision or condition of this Will should be held invalid, void, or inoperative, I direct that such invalidity shall not effect any other part, clause, provision or condition hereof this my Last Will and Testament. It is my intention that each of the separate provisions shall be independent of each of the others and that the remainder of this Will shall be strictly enforced as though such part, provision or condition had not been contained herein.

I, _____ **John Michael Doe** _____, the Testator, sign my name to this instrument this **21** day of _____ **March** _____, **1999**, and being first duly sworn, do hereby declare to the undersigned authority that I sign and execute this instrument as my Last Will and Testament and that I sign it willingly, that I execute it as my free and voluntary act for the purposes therein expressed, and that I am eighteen (18) years of age or older, of sound mind, and under no constraint or undue influence.

Signature
_____
signature

WITNESSES

We, _____ **First Witness (print name)** _____, **Second Witness (print name)** _____,

and _____ **Third Witness (print name)** _____, the witnesses, sign our names to this instrument, being first duly sworn and do hereby declare to the undersigned authority that the testator signs and executes this instrument as his Last Will and Testament and that he signs it willingly, and that each of us, in the presence and hearing of the testator and in the presence of the other subscribing witnesses, hereby signs this Last Will and Testament as witnesses to the testator's signing, and that to the best of our knowledge the testator is eighteen (18) years of age or older, of sound mind, and under no constraint or undue influence.

(witness signatures)   (witness address, city, state)

_____ **First Witness Signature** _____ residing at _____ **263 Oak Street** _____

_____ **Witness City/State/Zip** _____

_____ **Second Witness Signature** _____ residing at _____ **1996 E. Pleasant Ave., Apt. B** _____

_____ **Witness City/State/Zip** _____

_____ **Third Witness Signature** _____ residing at _____ **1466 S. 51st Street** _____

_____ **Witness City/State/Zip** _____

EIGHTH: Headings. The headings of the various items of this Will are included only in order to make it easier to locate the subject covered under each provision and are not to be used in construing this Will or in ascertaining my intentions.

NINTH: Governing Laws. This Will is executed and is to be construed in accordance with the

page **3** of **5**   **Your Initials**

WILL WITHOUT MINOR CHILDREN - SAMPLE

laws of the State of _____ **Your State** _____ and the dispositions

made under this Will are to be construed in accordance with the laws of the State of

_____ **Your State** _____ .

IN WITNESS WHEREOF, I, _____ **John Michael Doe** _____ , sign,

publish, and declare this instrument, consisting of __**5**__ pages, each of which has been initialed

by me, to be my Last Will and Testament in the presence of the persons witnessing it at my

request on this __**21**__ day of _____ **March** _____ , __**1999**__ , in

_____ **Your County** _____ County, _____ **Your State** _____ .

_____
Signature
signature

WITNESSES

The foregoing instrument, consisting of __**5**__ pages, was, on the date stated above, signed,

published, and declared by _____ **John Michael Doe** _____ to

be his/her Last Will and Testament in our presence and we, at his/her request and in his/her

presence and in the presence of each other, subscribe our names as attesting witnesses this

__**21**__ day of _____ **March** _____ , __**1999**__ , in _____ **Your County** _____

County, _____ **Your State** _____ .

(witness signatures)   (witness address, city, state)

First Witness Signature	residing at	**263 Oak Street**
		Witness City/State/Zip
Second Witness Signature	residing at	**1996 E. Pleasant Ave., Apt. B**
		Witness City/State/Zip
Third Witness Signature	residing at	**1466 S. 51st Street**
		Witness City/State/Zip

page __**4**__ of __**5**__   **Your Initials**

NOTARIZATION

State of _____ **Your State** _____, County of _____ **Your County** _____ (ss.)

Subscribed, sworn to and acknowledged before me by _____ **John Michael Doe** _____

_____ the testator, and subscribed and sworn to before me by

_____ **First Witness (print name)** _____, **Second Witness (print name)**

_____, and _____ **Third Witness (print name)** _____

witnesses, who proved to me, with satisfactory evidence, to be the person whose name is

subscribed to this instrument and acknowledged signing the foregoing Last Will and Testament

and the same is the above's free act and deed.

IN TESTIMONY WHEREOF, I have hereunto subscribed my name and affixed my Notarial Seal

at _____ **Your County** _____, _____ **Your State** _____ this **21** day of

_____ **March** _____, **1999** .

My commission expires _____ **4/16/2001** _____   _____ **Notary's Signature** _____
                                                                                                          Signature of Notary Public

page **5** of **5**   **Your Initials**

Last Will and Testament

of

_____

I, _____ now domiciled of

_____ County, State of _____,
being now of sound mind, memory and understanding, do make, publish and declare this to be
my LAST WILL AND TESTAMENT, hereby revoking and making null and void any and all prior
Last Wills and Testaments and Codicils heretofore made by me. All references herein to this
Will shall be construed as referring to this Will only.

FIRST: I hereby direct that all my just debts and obligations, including my funeral expenses and
the cost of the administration of my estate, be paid as soon after my death as practical, excepting
any mortgage indebtedness or other long-term contractual indebtedness secured either by real
or personal property, both which may exist as a part of this my estate and may be continued and
assumed by the beneficiary of said property. My Executor/trix, with the proper discretion, may
pay from my domiciliary estate all or any portion of the cost of ancillary administration and similar
proceeding in other jurisdictions.

I direct that my Executor/trix pay out of my estate all inheritance, estate, succession, and other
taxes by whatever name called (together with any penalty thereon), assessed by reason of my
death with regard to all properties and assets subject to such taxes, whether or not such taxes
would be payable by any other recipient or beneficiary or possessor of such property in the
absence of this provision. Contribution or reimbursement on account of any such taxes shall not
be collected from any such beneficiary or possessor provided that my estate is sufficient to pay
such taxes.

SECOND: I give, devise, and bequeath of this my estate, to each of the below-named
beneficiaries specific gifts of personal property, as follows:

a) I give _____

_____ to my

_____, _____ of

_____ of if s/he (it) fails to survive

me by thirty (30) days, to my _____, _____,

of _____.

b) I give _____

_____ to my

_____, _____ of

_____ of if s/he (it) fails to survive

me by thirty (30) days, to my _____, _____,

of _____.

page _____ of _____   _____

THIRD: I give, devise and bequeath of this my estate, to the below-named beneficiaries specific cash gifts, as follows:

a) I give _____ Dollars ($_____ to

my _____, _____

_____ or if

s/he (it) fails to survive me by thirty (30) days, to my _____,

_____ of _____

_____.

b) I give _____ Dollars ($_____) to

my _____, _____, of

_____ or if

s/he (it) fails to survive me by thirty (30) days, to my _____,

_____ of _____

_____.

FOURTH: All the rest and remainder of my estate, whether real, personal, and mixed, or whatever kind of nature, and wheresoever situated, including all property which I may acquire or become entitled to after the execution of this Will, remaining after payment of my debts, funeral expenses, taxes, administration costs and individual bequests, I give, devise and bequeath

to my _____, _____,

of _____.

In the event s/he has predeceased me or we both die as the result of a common disaster, then

I give, devise and bequeath my estate to my _____,

_____, of _____

_____.

Should any such beneficiary named in Article Four predecease me, then his or her share shall pass per stirpes, that is: (a) if that beneficiary has living issue, the portion of my estate otherwise reserved for that beneficiary shall be distributed among said living issue by right of representation; or (b) if that beneficiary has no living issue, the portion of my estate otherwise reserved for that beneficiary shall be distributed among those of my beneficiaries who did survive me by right of representation.

FIFTH: In the event that any person named in this Last Will and Testament shall fail to survive my death by thirty (30) days, it shall be presumed that they failed to survive me.

SIXTH: I appoint my _____, _____ of

_____, to be the Executor/trix of this my Last Will and Testament, to serve without bond. If s/he shall predecease me or, for any reason, fail to serve to Executor/trix, then in such event, I appoint my _____,

_____ of _____

to serve as Executor/trix without bond.

page _____ of _____   _____

SEVENTH: In the event, any part, clause, provision or condition of this Will should be held invalid, void, or inoperative, I direct that such invalidity shall not effect any other part, clause, provision or condition hereof this my Last Will and Testament. It is my intention that each of the separate provisions shall be independent of each of the others and that the remainder of this Will shall be strictly enforced as though such part, provision or condition had not been contained herein.

I, _____, the Testator, sign my name to this instrument this _____ day of _____, _____, and being first duly sworn, do hereby declare to the undersigned authority that I sign and execute this instrument as my Last Will and Testament and that I sign it willingly, that I execute it as my free and voluntary act for the purposes therein expressed, and that I am eighteen (18) years of age or older, of sound mind, and under no constraint or undue influence.

_____
signature

WITNESSES

We, _____, _____,

and _____, the witnesses, sign our names to this instrument, being first duly sworn and do hereby declare to the undersigned authority that the testator signs and executes this instrument as his Last Will and Testament and that he signs it willingly, and that each of us, in the presence and hearing of the testator and in the presence of the other subscribing witnesses, hereby signs this Last Will and Testament as witnesses to the testator's signing, and that to the best of our knowledge the testator is eighteen (18) years of age or older, of sound mind, and under no constraint or undue influence.

(witness signatures)   (witness address, city, state)

_____ residing at _____

_____

_____ residing at _____

_____

_____ residing at _____

_____

EIGHTH: Headings. The headings of the various items of this Will are included only in order to make it easier to locate the subject covered under each provision and are not to be used in construing this Will or in ascertaining my intentions.

NINTH: Governing Laws. This Will is executed and is to be construed in accordance with the

page _____ of _____   _____

laws of the State of _____ and the dispositions

made under this Will are to be construed in accordance with the laws of the State of

_____.

IN WITNESS WHEREOF, I, _____, sign,

publish, and declare this instrument, consisting of _____ pages, each of which has been initialed

by me, to be my Last Will and Testament in the presence of the persons witnessing it at my

request on this _____ day of _____, _____, in

_____ County, _____.

_____
signature

WITNESSES

The foregoing instrument, consisting of _____ pages, was, on the date stated above, signed,

published, and declared by _____ to

be his/her Last Will and Testament in our presence and we, at his/her request and in his/her

presence and in the presence of each other, subscribe our names as attesting witnesses this

_____ day of _____, _____, in _____

County, _____.

(witness signatures)   (witness address, city, state)

_____ residing at _____

_____

_____ residing at _____

_____

_____ residing at _____

_____

page _____ of _____   _____

NOTARIZATION

State of _____, County of _____ (ss.)

Subscribed, sworn to and acknowledged before me by _____

_____ the testator, and subscribed and sworn to before me by

_____, _____

_____, and _____

witnesses, who proved to me, with satisfactory evidence, to be the person whose name is

subscribed to this instrument and acknowledged signing the foregoing Last Will and Testament

and the same is the above's free act and deed.

IN TESTIMONY WHEREOF, I have hereunto subscribed my name and affixed my Notarial Seal

at _____, _____ this_____ day of

_____, _____.

My commission expires _____   _____
                                                    Signature of Notary Public

page _____ of _____   _____

BLANK FORMS

Last Will and Testament With Minor Children

Forms are perforated for easy removal. Fold carefully and tear along the perforation to remove pages.

Last Will and Testament

of

Joseph Allen Jones

I, _____**Joseph Allen Jones**_____ now domiciled of _____**Your**_____ County, State of _____**Your**_____,
being now of sound mind, memory and understanding, do make, publish and declare this to be my **LAST WILL AND TESTAMENT**, hereby revoking and making null and void any and all prior Last Wills and Testaments and Codicils heretofore made by me. All references herein to this Will shall be construed as referring to this Will only.

FIRST: I hereby direct that all my just debts and obligations, including my funeral expenses and the cost of the administration of my estate, be paid as soon after my death as practical, excepting any mortgage indebtedness or other long-term contractual indebtedness secured either by real or personal property, both which may exist as a part of this my estate and may be continued and assumed by the beneficiary of said property. My Executor/trix, with the proper discretion, may pay from my domiciliary estate all or any portion of the cost of ancillary administration and similar proceeding in other jurisdictions.

I direct that my Executor/trix pay out of my estate all inheritance, estate, succession, and other taxes by whatever name called (together with any penalty thereon), assessed by reason of my death with regard to all properties and assets subject to such taxes, whether or not such taxes would be payable by any other recipient or beneficiary or possessor of such property in the absence of this provision. Contribution or reimbursement on account of any such taxes shall not be collected from any such beneficiary or possessor provided that my estate is sufficient to pay such taxes.

SECOND: I give, devise, and bequeath of this my estate, to each of the below-named beneficiaries specific gifts of personal property, as follows:

a) I give _____**my father's gold pocket watch which has been in my family for three generations and 1000 shares of XYZ Company common stock**_____ to my _____**son**_____, _____**Edward Arnold Jones**_____ of _____**2007 South Street, His City, His State**_____ of if s/he (it) fails to survive me by thirty (30) days, to my _____**son**_____, _____**Matthew Adam Jones**_____, of _____**6161 Maple Avenue, His City, His State**_____.

b) I give (it) _____**my 1977 Ford T-Bird Serial Number 0344583 and 1000 shares of ABC company common stock**_____ to my _____**son**_____, _____**Matthew Adam Jones**_____ of _____**6161 Maple Street, His City, His State**_____ of if s/he(it) fails to survive me by thirty (30) days, to my _____**son**_____, _____**Edward Arnold Jones**_____, of _____**2007 South Street, His City, His State**_____.

page __1__ of __5__   **Your Initials**

WILL WITH MINOR CHILDREN - SAMPLE

THIRD: I give, devise and bequeath of this my estate, to the below-named beneficiaries specific cash gifts, as follows:

a) I give _____ **Five Thousand and zero cents** _____ Dollars

($ **5,000**) to my _____ **college** _____, _____ **The University for All** _____,

of _____ **300 Education Avenue, Its City, Its State** _____ or

if s/he (it) fails to survive me by thirty (30) days, to my _____ **brother** _____,

_____ **Earl James Jones** _____ of _____

_____ **10 Sunshine Blvd., His City, His State** _____.

b) I give _____ **One Thousand and Five Hundred and zero cents** _____ Dollars

($ **1,500**) to my _____ **good friend** _____, _____ **John Quincy Doe** _____,

of _____ **8844 Goodtimes Avenue, His City, His State** _____ or

if s/he (it) fails to survive me by thirty (30) days, to my _____ **brother** _____,

_____ **Earl James Jones** _____ of _____

_____ **10 Sunshine Blvd., His City, His State** _____.

FOURTH: All the rest and remainder of my estate, whether real, personal, and mixed, or whatever kind of nature, and wheresoever situated, including all property which I may acquire or become entitled to after the execution of this Will, remaining after payment of my debts, funeral expenses, taxes, administration costs and individual bequests, I give, devise and bequeath

to my _____ **wife** _____, _____ **Cynthia Davis Jones** _____,

of _____ **33 Maple Avenue, Her City, Her State** _____.

In the event s/he has predeceased me or we both die as the result of a common disaster, then

I give, devise and bequeath my estate to my _____ **children (in equal shares)** _____,

_____ **Edward Arnold Jones and Matthew Adam Jones** _____, of _____ **2007 Second** _____

_____ **Street, His City, His State and 6161 Maple Avenue, His City, His State** _____.

Should any such beneficiary named in Article Four predecease me, then his or her share shall pass per stirpes, that is: (a) if that beneficiary has living issue, the portion of my estate otherwise reserved for that beneficiary shall be distributed among said living issue by right of representation; or (b) if that beneficiary has no living issue, the portion of my estate otherwise reserved for that beneficiary shall be distributed among those of my beneficiaries who did survive me by right of representation.

FIFTH: In the event that any person named in this Last Will and Testament shall fail to survive my death by thirty (30) days, it shall be presumed that they failed to survive me.

SIXTH: I appoint my _____ **wife** _____, _____ **Cynthia Davis Jones** _____,

of _____ **33 Maple Avenue, Her City, Her State** _____ to be

the Executor/trix of this my Last Will and Testament, to serve without bond. If s/he shall

predecease me or, for any reason, fail to serve to Executor/trix, then in such event, I appoint my

_____ **brother** _____, _____ **Earl James Jones** _____ of

_____ **10 Sunshine Blvd., His City, His State** _____

to serve as Executor/trix without bond.

page **2** of **5** **Your Initials** _____

SEVENTH: I designate and appoint my _____**wife**_____, **Cynthia Davis Williams** **Jones** of _____**33 Maple Avenue, Her City, Her State**_____ as the Guardian of the person and property of my minor child/ren. In the event that the above-appointed Guardian shall not be able to serve as Guardian for any reason, I designate and appoint my _____**brother**_____, _____**Earl James Jones**_____ of _____**10 Sunshine Blvd., His City, His State**_____ as the Guardian of the person and property of my minor child/ren.

a) To the extent permitted by law, I direct that no such person named as Guardian in this Last Will and Testament be required to file a bond or other security for the faithful performance of his/her duties as Guardian of the estate of my minor child/ren.

b) It is my desire that the loving care and treatment of my minor child/ren be trusted to the person designated by me as Guardian of my minor child/ren. I desire the above-named Guardian to exercise reasonable and broad discretion in dealing both with the person and property of my minor child/ren, including performing all acts, taking all proceedings and exercising all such rights and privileges with relation to any matter affecting both the person and property of my minor child/ren, although not specifically mentioned in this Will.

EIGHTH: In the event, any part, clause, provision or condition of this Will should be held invalid, void, or inoperative, I direct that such invalidity shall not effect any other part, clause, provision or condition hereof this my Last Will and Testament. It is my intention that each of the separate provisions shall be independent of each of the others and that the remainder of this Will shall be strictly enforced as though such part, provision or condition had not been contained herein.

I, _____**Joseph Allen Jones**_____, the Testator, sign my name to this instrument this **21** day of _____**March**_____, **1999**, and being first duly sworn, do hereby declare to the undersigned authority that I sign and execute this instrument as my Last Will and Testament and that I sign it willingly, that I execute it as my free and voluntary act for the purposes therein expressed, and that I am eighteen (18) years of age or older, of sound mind, and under no constraint or undue influence.

Signature
signature

WITNESSES

We, _____**First Witness (print name)**_____, _____**Second Witness (print name)**_____, and _____**Third Witness (print name)**_____, the witnesses, sign our names to this instrument, being first duly sworn and do hereby declare to the undersigned authority that the testator signs and executes this instrument as his Last Will and Testament and that he signs it willingly, and that each of us, in the presence and hearing of the testator and in the presence of the other subscribing witnesses, hereby signs this Last Will and Testament as witnesses to the testator's signing, and that to the best of our knowledge the testator is eighteen (18) years of age or older, of sound mind, and under no constraint or undue influence.

WILL WITH MINOR CHILDREN - SAMPLE

(witness signatures)   (witness address, city, state)

First Witness Signature _____ residing at _____ **447 N. First Street** _____

_____ . _____ **Witness City/State/Zip** _____

Second Witness Signature _____ residing at _____ **8009 CR 146** _____

_____ _____ **Witness City/State/Zip** _____

Third Witness Signature _____ residing at _____ **927 S. 93rd Avenue** _____

_____ _____ **Witness City/State/Zip** _____

NINTH: Headings. The headings of the various items of this Will are included only in order to make it easier to locate the subject covered under each provision and are not to be used in construing this Will or in ascertaining my intentions.

TENTH: Governing Laws. This Will is executed and is to be construed in accordance with the laws of the State of _____ **Your State** _____ and the dispositions made under this Will are to be construed in accordance with the laws of the State of _____ **Your State** _____ .

IN WITNESS WHEREOF, I, _____ **Joseph Allen Jones** _____ , sign, publish, and declare this instrument, consisting of ___ **5** ___ pages, each of which has been initialed by me, to be my Last Will and Testament in the presence of the persons witnessing it at my request on this ___ **21** ___ day of _____ **March** _____ , ___ **1999** ___ , in _____ **Your County** _____ County, _____ **Your State** _____ .

_____
Signature
signature

WITNESSES

The foregoing instrument, consisting of ___ **5** ___ pages, was, on the date stated above, signed, published, and declared by _____ **Joseph Allen Jones** _____ to be his/her Last Will and Testament in our presence and we, at his/her request and in his/her

page ___ **4** ___ of ___ **5** ___   **Your Initials** presence and in the presence of each other, subscribe our names as attesting witnesses this

__21__ day of _____ **March** _____ , __1999__ , in _____ **Your County** _____

County, _____ **Your State** _____ .

(witness signatures)   (witness address, city, state)

_____ **First Witness Signature** _____ residing at _____ **447 N. First Street** _____

Witness City / State / Zip

_____ **Second Witness Signature** _____ residing at _____ **8009 CR 146** _____

Witness City / State / Zip

_____ **Third Witness Signature** _____ residing at _____ **927 S. 93rd Avenue** _____

Witness City / State / Zip

NOTARIZATION

State of _____ **Your State** _____ , County of _____ **Your County** _____ (ss.)

Subscribed, sworn to and acknowledged before me by _____ **Joseph Allen Doe** _____

_____ the testator, and subscribed and sworn to before me by

_____ **First Witness (print name)** _____ , **Second Witness (print name)**

_____ , and _____ **Third Witness (print name)** _____

witnesses, who proved to me, with satisfactory evidence, to be the person whose name is

subscribed to this instrument and acknowledged signing the foregoing Last Will and Testament

and the same is the above's free act and deed.

IN TESTIMONY WHEREOF, I have hereunto subscribed my name and affixed my Notarial Seal

at _____ **Your County** _____ , _____ **Your State** _____ this __21__ day of

_____ **March** _____ , __1999__ .

My commission expires _____ **8/16/2003** _____   _____ **Notary's Signature** _____
Signature of Notary Public

page __5__ of __5__   **Your Initials**

Last Will and Testament

of

_____

I, _____ now domiciled of

_____ County, State of _____,
being now of sound mind, memory and understanding, do make, publish and declare this to be
my **LAST WILL AND TESTAMENT**, hereby revoking and making null and void any and all prior
Last Wills and Testaments and Codicils heretofore made by me. All references herein to this
Will shall be construed as referring to this Will only.

FIRST: I hereby direct that all my just debts and obligations, including my funeral expenses and
the cost of the administration of my estate, be paid as soon after my death as practical, excepting
any mortgage indebtedness or other long-term contractual indebtedness secured either by real
or personal property, both which may exist as a part of this my estate and may be continued and
assumed by the beneficiary of said property. My Executor/trix, with the proper discretion, may
pay from my domiciliary estate all or any portion of the cost of ancillary administration and similar
proceeding in other jurisdictions.

I direct that my Executor/trix pay out of my estate all inheritance, estate, succession, and other
taxes by whatever name called (together with any penalty thereon), assessed by reason of my
death with regard to all properties and assets subject to such taxes, whether or not such taxes
would be payable by any other recipient or beneficiary or possessor of such property in the
absence of this provision. Contribution or reimbursement on account of any such taxes shall not
be collected from any such beneficiary or possessor provided that my estate is sufficient to pay
such taxes.

SECOND: I give, devise, and bequeath of this my estate, to each of the below-named
beneficiaries specific gifts of personal property, as follows:

a) I give _____

_____ to my

_____, _____ of

_____ of if s/he (it) fails to survive

me by thirty (30) days, to my _____, _____,

of _____.

b) I give _____

_____ to my

_____, _____ of

_____ of if s/he(it) fails to survive

me by thirty (30) days, to my _____, _____,

of _____.

page _____ of _____   _____

THIRD: I give, devise and bequeath of this my estate, to the below-named beneficiaries specific cash gifts, as follows:

a) I give _____ Dollars

($_____) to my _____, _____,

of _____

_____ or

if s/he (it) fails to survive me by thirty (30) days, to my _____,

_____ of _____

_____

_____.

b) I give _____ Dollars

($_____) to my _____, _____,

of _____

_____ or

if s/he (it) fails to survive me by thirty (30) days, to my _____,

_____ of _____

_____

_____.

FOURTH: All the rest and remainder of my estate, whether real, personal, and mixed, or whatever kind of nature, and wheresoever situated, including all property which I may acquire or become entitled to after the execution of this Will, remaining after payment of my debts, funeral expenses, taxes, administration costs and individual bequests, I give, devise and bequeath to my _____, _____,

of _____

_____.

In the event s/he has predeceased me or we both die as the result of a common disaster, then I give, devise and bequeath my estate to my _____,

_____, of _____

_____.

Should any such beneficiary named in Article Four predecease me, then his or her share shall pass per stirpes, that is: (a) if that beneficiary has living issue, the portion of my estate other-wise reserved for that beneficiary shall be distributed among said living issue by right of representation; or (b) if that beneficiary has no living issue, the portion of my estate otherwise reserved for that beneficiary shall be distributed among those of my beneficiaries who did survive me by right of representation.

FIFTH: In the event that any person named in this Last Will and Testament shall fail to survive my death by thirty (30) days, it shall be presumed that they failed to survive me.

SIXTH: I appoint my _____, _____,

of _____ to be

the Executor/trix of this my Last Will and Testament, to serve without bond. If s/he shall predecease me or, for any reason, fail to serve to Executor/trix, then in such event, I appoint my

_____, _____ of

_____ to

serve as Executor/trix without bond.

page _____ of _____

_____

SEVENTH: I designate and appoint my _____, _____
_____ of _____
as the Guardian of the person and property of my minor child/ren. In the event that the above-appointed Guardian shall not be able to serve as Guardian for any reason, I designate and appoint my _____, _____
of _____ as the Guardian of the person and property of my minor child/ren.

a) To the extent permitted by law, I direct that no such person named as Guardian in this Last Will and Testament be required to file a bond or other security for the faithful performance of his/her duties as Guardian of the estate of my minor child/ren.

b) It is my desire that the loving care and treatment of my minor child/ren be trusted to the person designated by me as Guardian of my minor child/ren. I desire the above-named Guardian to exercise reasonable and broad discretion in dealing both with the person and property of my minor child/ren, including performing all acts, taking all proceedings and exercising all such rights and privileges with relation to any matter affecting both the person and property of my minor child/ren, although not specifically mentioned in this Will.

EIGHTH: In the event, any part, clause, provision or condition of this Will should be held invalid, void, or inoperative, I direct that such invalidity shall not effect any other part, clause, provision or condition hereof this my Last Will and Testament. It is my intention that each of the separate provisions shall be independent of each of the others and that the remainder of this Will shall be strictly enforced as though such part, provision or condition had not been contained herein.

I, _____, the Testator,
sign my name to this instrument this _____ day of _____, _____, and being first duly sworn, do hereby declare to the undersigned authority that I sign and execute this instrument as my Last Will and Testament and that I sign it willingly, that I execute it as my free and voluntary act for the purposes therein expressed, and that I am eighteen (18) years of age or older, of sound mind, and under no constraint or undue influence.

_____
signature

WITNESSES

We, _____, _____,
and _____, the witnesses, sign our names to this instrument, being first duly sworn and do hereby declare to the undersigned authority that the testator signs and executes this instrument as his Last Will and Testament and that he signs it willingly, and that each of us, in the presence and hearing of the testator and in the presence of the other subscribing witnesses, hereby signs this Last Will and Testament as witnesses to the testator's signing, and that to the best of our knowledge the testator is eighteen (18) years of age or older, of sound mind, and under no constraint or undue influence.

page _____ of _____   _____

_____ residing at _____

_____

_____ residing at _____

_____

_____ residing at _____

_____

NINTH: Headings. The headings of the various items of this Will are included only in order to make it easier to locate the subject covered under each provision and are not to be used in construing this Will or in ascertaining my intentions.

TENTH: Governing Laws. This Will is executed and is to be construed in accordance with the laws of the State of _____ and the dispositions made under this Will are to be construed in accordance with the laws of the State of

_____.

IN WITNESS WHEREOF, I, _____, sign, publish, and declare this instrument, consisting of _____ pages, each of which has been initialed by me, to be my Last Will and Testament in the presence of the persons witnessing it at my request on this _____ day of _____, _____, in _____ County, _____.

_____
signature

WITNESSES

The foregoing instrument, consisting of _____ pages, was, on the date stated above, signed, published, and declared by _____ to be his/her Last Will and Testament in our presence and we, at his/her request and in his/her

page _____ of _____   _____

presence and in the presence of each other, subscribe our names as attesting witnesses this

_____ day of _____, _____, in _____

County, _____.

(witness signatures)   (witness address, city, state)

_____ residing at _____

_____

_____ residing at _____

_____

_____ residing at _____

_____

NOTARIZATION

State of _____, County of _____ (ss.)

Subscribed, sworn to and acknowledged before me by _____

_____ the testator, and subscribed and sworn to before me by

_____, _____

_____, and _____

witnesses, who proved to me, with satisfactory evidence, to be the person whose name is

subscribed to this instrument and acknowledged signing the foregoing Last Will and Testament

and the same is the above's free act and deed.

IN TESTIMONY WHEREOF, I have hereunto subscribed my name and affixed my Notarial Seal

at _____, _____ this_____ day of

_____, _____.

My commission expires _____   _____

                                                         Signature of Notary Public

page _____ of _____   _____

BLANK FORMS

Last Will and Testament

(to make and type yourself)

Forms are perforated for easy removal. Fold carefully and tear along the perforation to remove pages.

Last Will and Testament

of

_____
Your Name

I, Your Name, now domiciled of Your County, State of Your State, being now of sound mind, memory and understanding, do make, publish and declare this to be my Last Will and Testament, hereby revoking and making null and void any and all prior Last Wills and Testaments and Codicils heretofore made by me. All references herein to this Will shall be construed as referring to this Will only.

FIRST: I hereby direct that all my just debts and obligations, including my funeral expenses and the cost of administering my estate, be paid as soon after my death as practical, excepting any mortgage indebtedness or other long-term contractual indebted-ness secured either by real or personal property, or both, which may exist as a part of this my estate and may be continued and assumed by the beneficiary of said property. My Executor/trix, with the proper discretion, may pay from my domiciliary estate all of any portion of the cost of ancillary administration and similar proceeding in other jurisdictions.

I direct that my Executor/trix pay out of my estate all inheritance, estate, succession, and other taxes by whatever name called (together with any penalty thereon) assessed by reason of my death with regard to all properties and assets subject to such taxes, whether or not such taxes would be payable by any other recipient or beneficiary or possessor of such property in the absence of this provision. Contribution or reimbursement on account of any such taxes shall not be collected from any such beneficiary or possessor provided that my estate is sufficient to pay such taxes.

SECOND: I specifically direct that my son, John H. Nogood, be disinherited and receive nothing from my estate.

THIRD: I give, devise, and bequeath of this my estate to each of the below-named beneficiaries specific gifts of personal property as follows:

a) I give my father's gold pocket watch which has been in my family for three generations and 1,000 shares of XYZ Company common stock to my son, Edward Arnold Jones of 2007 Second Street, His City, His State or, if he fails to survive me by thirty (30) days, to my son, Matthew Adam Jones of 6161 Maple Avenue, His City, His State.

b) I give my 1958 T-Bird Serial Number 0344583 and 1,000 shares of ABC Company common stock to my son, Matthew Adam Jones of 6161 Maple Avenue, His

page __1__ of __6__   **Your Initials**

City, His State or, if he fails to survive me by thirty (30) days, to my son, Edward Arnold Jones of 2007 Second Street, His City, His State.

c) I give my complete coin collection and stamp collection to my daughter, Mary Ann Jones of 33 Maple Avenue, Her City, Her State or, if she fails to survive me by thirty (30) days, to my wife, Cynthia Davis Williams Jones of 33 Maple Avenue, Her City, Her State.

d) I give my golf clubs and golf cart to my friend, Andrew Howard Stone of 4200 N. Oak Blvd., His City, His State or, if he fails to survive me by thirty (30) days, to my son, Edward Arnold Jones of 2007 Second Street, His City, His State.

FOURTH: I give, devise, and bequeath of this my estate, to the below-named beneficiaries specific cash gifts, as follows:

a) I give Five Thousand and zero cents Dollars ($5,000) to my college, The University for All of 300 Education Avenue, Its City, Its State or if it fails to survive me by thirty (30) days, to my brother, Earl James Jones of 10 Sunshine Blvd., His City, His State.

b) I give One Thousand and zero cents Dollars ($1,000) to my good friend, John Quincy Doe of 8844 Goodtimes Avenue, His City, His State or, if he fails to survive me by thirty (30) days, to my wife, Cynthia Davis Jones of 33 Maple Avenue, Her City, Her State.

c) I give One Thousand and zero cents Dollars ($2,000) to each of my children, Edward Arnold Jones 2007 Second Street, His City, His State; Matthew Adam Jones of 6161 Maple Avenue, His City, His State; and Mary Ann Jones of 33 Maple Avenue, Her City, Her State; or, if they fail to survive me by thirty (30) days, to my wife, Cynthia Davis Jones of 33 Maple Avenue, Her City, Her State.

d) I give Two Thousand and Five Hundred and zero cents Dollars ($2,500) to my church, The Church for All of 2301 North High Street, Its City, Its State; or if it fails to survive me by thirty (30) days, to my wife, Cynthia Davis Jones of 33 Maple Avenue, Her City, Her State.

FIFTH: I give, devise, and bequeath of this my estate, to each of the below-named beneficiaries specific gifts of real property, as follows:

a) I give the real property commonly known as Lot 641, Mountain View Resorts, according to the records of the Lake County Recorder, State of Kentucky, to my son, Matthew Adam Jones of 6161 Maple Avenue, His City, His State, or, if he fails to survive me by thirty (30) days, to my wife, Cynthia Davis Jones of 33 Maple Avenue, Her City, Her State.

SIXTH: All the rest, residue and remainder of my estate, whether real, person and mixed, of whatever kind and nature and wheresoever situated, including all

page ___**2**___ of ___**6**___   **Your Initials** property which I may acquire or become entitled to after the execution of this Will, remaining after payment of my debts, funeral expenses, taxes, administration costs and individual bequests, I give, devise and bequeath to my beloved wife, Cynthia Davis Jones of 33 Maple Avenue, Her City, Her State.

In the event she predeceased me or we both die as the result of a common disaster, then I give, devise and bequeath the residue of my estate to my children, in equal shares, Edward Arnold Jones, Matthew Adam Jones, and Mary Ann Jones.

Should any such beneficiary named in Article Six predecease me, then his or her share shall pass per stirpes, in equal shares, that is: (a) if that beneficiary has living issue, the portion of my estate otherwise reserved for that beneficiary shall be distributed among said living issue by right of representation; or (b) if that beneficiary has no living issue, the portion of my estate otherwise reserved for that beneficiary shall be distributed among those of my beneficiaries who did survive me by right of representation.

SEVENTH: In the event that any person or organization named in the Last Will and Testament shall fail to survive my death by thirty (30) days, it shall be presumed that they fail to survive me.

EIGHTH: I appoint my beloved wife, Cynthia Davis Jones of 33 Maple Avenue, Her City, Her State, to be the Executrix of this my Last Will and Testament, to serve without bond. If she shall predecease me or, for any reason, fail to serve as Executrix, then in such event, I appoint my brother, Earl James Jones of 10 Sunshine Blvd., His City, His State, to serve as executor without bond.

I vest my Executor/trix with full power and discretion, without any court order or proceeding, to sell, pursuant to option or otherwise public or private sale and upon such items as s/he should deem best, any real or person property belonging to my estate without regard to the necessity of such sale for purpose paying debts, taxes, or legacies or to retain any such property not so required, without liability for any depreciation thereof; to adjust, compromise, and settle all matters of business and claims in favor of or against my estate; and to do any and all things necessary or proper to complete the administration of my estate, all as fully as I could do if living.

NINTH: I designate and appoint my wife, Cynthia Davis Jones of 33 Maple Avenue, Her City, Her State, as the Guardian of the person and property of my minor child. In the event that the above-appointed Guardian shall not be able to serve as Guardian, for any reason, I designate and appoint my brother, Earl James Jones of 10 Sunshine Blvd., His City, His State, as the Guardian of the person and property of my minor child.

b)   It is my desire that the loving care and treatment of my minor child be trusted to the person designated by me as Guardian of my minor child. I desire the above-

page ___**3**___ of ___**6**___   **Your Initials** named Guardian to exercise reasonable and broad discretion in dealing both with the person and property of my minor child so as to be able to do everything deemed advisable the best interest of my minor child, including performing all acts, taking all proceedings and exercising all such rights and privileges with relation to any matter affecting both the person and property of my minor child, although not specifically mentioned in this Will.

TENTH: In the event any part, clause, provision or condition of this Will should be held invalid, void, or inoperative, I direct that such invalidity shall not effect any other part, clause, provision or condition hereof this my Last Will and Testament. It is my intention that each of the separate provisions shall be independent of each of the others and that the remainder of this Will shall be strictly enforced as though such part, provision or condition had not been contained herein.

I, _____ **Your Name** _____ , the Testator, sign my name to this instrument this **day** day of _____ **month** _____ , **year** , and being first duly sworn, do hereby declare to the undersigned authority that I sign and execute this instrument as my Last Will and Testament and that I sign it willingly, that I execute it as my free and voluntary act for the purposes therein expressed, and that I am eighteen (18) years of age or older, of sound mind, and under no constraint or undue influence.

_____
Your Signature

WITNESSES

We , _____ **First Witness (print name)** _____ , _____ **Second Witness (print name)** _____ ,

and _____ **Third Witness (print name)** _____ , the witnesses, sign our names to this instrument, being first duly sworn and do hereby declare to the undersigned authority that the testator signs and executes this instrument as his Last Will and Testament and that he signs it willingly, and that each of us, in the presence and hearing of the testator and in the presence of the other subscribing witnesses, hereby signs this Last Will and Testament as witnesses to the testator's signing, and that to the best of our knowledge the testator is eighteen (18) years of age or older, of sound mind, and under no constraint or undue influence.

(witness signatures)   (witness address, city, state)

_____ **First Witness Signature** _____ residing at _____ **Witness Address** _____

_____
Witness City/State/Zip

page __ **4** __ of __ **6** __   **Your Initials**

__Second Witness Signature__	residing at	__Witness Address__
		__Witness City/State/Zip__
__Third Witness Signature__	residing at	__Witness Address__
		__Witness City/State/Zip__

ELEVENTH: Headings. The headings of the various items of this Will are included only in order to make it easier to locate the subject covered under each provision and are not to be used in construing this Will or in ascertaining my intentions.

TWELFTH: Governing Laws. This Will is executed and is to be construed in accordance with the laws of the State of __Your State__

and the dispositions made under this Will are to be construed in accordance with the laws of the State of __Your State__.

IN WITNESS WHEREOF, I, __Your Name__, sign, publish, and declare this instrument, consisting of __6__ pages, each of which has been initialed by me, to be my Last Will and Testament in the presence of the persons witnessing it at my request on this __day__ day of __month__, __year__, in __Your County__ County, __Your State__.

__Your Signature__
signature

WITNESSES

The foregoing instrument, consisting of __6__ pages, was, on the date stated above, signed, published, and declared by __Your Name__ to be his/her Last Will and Testament in our presence and we, at his/her request and in his/her presence and in the presence of each other, subscribe our names as attesting witnesses this __day__ day of __month__, __year__,

page __5__ of __6__   __Your Initials__ in _____**Your County**_____ County, _____**Your State**_____ .

(witness signatures)	(witness address, city, state)
_____**First Witness Signature**_____ residing at	_____**Witness Street Address**_____
	Witness City/State
_____**Second Witness Signature**_____ residing at	_____**Witness Street Address**_____
	Witness City/State
_____**Third Witness Signature**_____ residing at	_____**Witness Street Address**_____
	Witness City/State

NOTARIZATION

State of _____**Your State**_____, County of _____**Your County**_____ (ss.)

Subscribed, sworn to and acknowledged before me by _____**Your Name**_____

_____ the testator, and subscribed and sworn to before me by

_____**First Witness (print name)**_____, _____**Second Witness (print name)**_____,

and _____**Third Witness (print name)**_____, witnesses, who proved to me, with

satisfactory evidence, to be the person whose name is subscribed to this

instrument and acknowledged signing the foregoing Last Will and Testament

and the same is the above's free act and deed.

IN TESTIMONY WHEREOF, I have hereunto subscribed my name and affixed

my Notarial Seal at _____**Your County**_____, _____**Your State**_____

this __**day**__ day of _____**month**_____, _____**year**_____ .

My commission expires _____**date/year**_____ _____**Notary's Signature**_____

Signature of Notary Public

page __**6**__ of __**6**__   **Your Initials**

Last Will and Testament

of
_____

I,

_____

b.

I, _____, the Testator, sign my name to this instrument this _____ day of _____, _____, and being first duly sworn, do hereby declare to the undersigned authority that I sign and execute this instrument as my Last Will and Testament and that I sign it willingly, that I execute it as my free and voluntary act for the purposes therein expressed, and that I am eighteen (18) years of age or older, of sound mind, and under no constraint or undue influence.

_____

WITNESSES

We, _____, _____,

and _____, the witnesses, sign our names to this instrument, being first duly sworn and do hereby declare to the undersigned authority that the testator signs and executes this instrument as his Last Will and Testament and that he signs it willingly, and that each of us, in the presence and hearing of the testator and in the presence of the other subscribing witnesses, hereby signs this Last Will and Testament as witnesses to the testator's signing, and that to the best of our knowledge the testator is eighteen (18) years of age or older, of sound mind, and under no constraint or undue influence.

(witness signatures)   (witness address, city, state)

_____ residing at _____

_____

_____ residing at _____

_____

_____ residing at _____

_____

_____: Headings. The headings of the various items of this Will are included only in order to make it easier to locate the subject covered under each provision and are not to be used in construing this Will or in ascertaining my intentions.

page _____ of _____   _____

_____: Governing Laws. This Will is executed and is to be construed in accordance with the laws of the State of _____ and the dispositions made under this Will are to be construed in accordance with the laws of the State of _____.

IN WITNESS WHEREOF, I, _____, sign, publish, and declare this instrument, consisting of _____ pages, each of which has been initialed by me, to be my Last Will and Testament in the presence of the persons witnessing it at my request on this _____ day of _____, _____, in _____ County, _____.

_____

WITNESSES

The foregoing instrument, consisting of _____ pages, was, on the date stated above, signed, published, and declared by _____ to be his/her Last Will and Testament in our presence and we, at his/her request and in his/her presence and in the presence of each other, subscribe our names as attesting witnesses this _____ day of _____, _____, in _____ County, _____.

(witness signatures)

(witness address, city, state)

_____ residing at _____

_____

_____ residing at _____

_____

page _____ of _____

_____

_____ residing at _____

_____

NOTARIZATION

State of _____, County of _____ (ss.)

Subscribed, sworn to and acknowledged before me by _____

_____ the testator, and subscribed and sworn to before me by

_____, _____,

and _____, witnesses, who proved to me, with

satisfactory evidence, to be the person whose name is subscribed to this

instrument and acknowledged signing the foregoing Last Will and Testament

and the same is the above's free act and deed.

IN TESTIMONY WHEREOF, I have hereunto subscribed my name and affixed

my Notarial Seal at _____, _____

this _____ day of _____, _____.

My commission expires _____ _____
                                        Signature of Notary Public

page _____ of _____   _____

Checklist

This is a checklist of the steps you should take in doing your own Last Will and Testament.

- [ ] You are certain you meet all the necessary requirements:
  - You are at least eighteen years of age and are considered to be a legal adult.
  - You are a legal resident of the United States and consider the state named in your address as your permanent home.
  - You are legally sane.

- [ ] You have decided on the following:
  - How you wish to divide your property.
  - Who you wish to appoint as your Executor/trix.
  - Who you wish to name as Guardian of your minor children.

- [ ] You have typed all forms necessary to complete your Last Will and Testament. (You have used your full legal names and those of your beneficiaries, Executor/trix(es), and Guardian(s), and have provided the name of your county.

- [ ] You have proofed your Last Will and Testament to be sure all the information is correct.

- [ ] You have signed your Last Will and Testament in the presence of at least two witnesses (or three, if required in your state) who are not named in your will.

- [ ] You have told your first- and second-choice Executors where you have placed your Last Will and Testament.

- [ ] You have reviewed your Will with an attorney (if you wish to do so or there are complicated circumstances affecting the division of your property).

You have now completed your Last Will and Testament. Congratulations! Please keep it in a safe place and make sure your Executor/trix has access to it. Remember, you must not alter your will by inserting handwritten or typed additions or changes. This will probably invalidate the entire will. State laws require that to make any changes to your will, you must go through the entire formal procedure again by drafting and signing your will and having your signature witnessed, or you must add a witnessed codicil or amendment (formal addition) to your old will. The codicil must also be signed in the presence of witnesses, who must add their signatures.

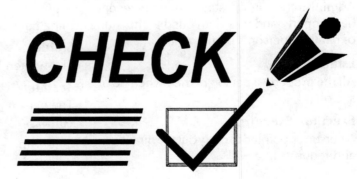

Explanation of Terms

Adult
A person 18 years of age or older in most states. (A few states require a person to be 21 years of age in order to leave real estate in a will.)

AKA
Also known as

Ancillary
Administration in state where decedent has real estate property and which is other than where decedent was domiciled

Beneficiary
A person or organization named in your will to inherit your property after the will is approved by a probate court

Bequeath
To give personal property in a will

Bond
A document which guarantees that a certain amount of money will be paid to those damaged if an executor, trustee, or guardian does not carry out their legal responsibilities

Codicil
A separate document (amendment) which is an addition to your will after the will has been written; (the codicil must be signed and witnessed like the will)

Decedent
A deceased person

Devise
To give real estate in a will

Domiciliary
Administration in the state where decedent has property and was domiciled at the time of death; a person's permanent home

Estate
All the property a person owned when he or she died

Executor/Executrix
A person appointed to carry out the directions and requests in a will

Guardian
A person appointed to care for and manage the estate and person of a minor child

Heir
A person who inherits property if there is no will

Holographic Will
A will entirely written, dated and signed by the testator in his own handwriting (legal in 25 states, but very difficult to probate)

Last Will and Testament (Will)
The instrument which ultimately fixes the disposition (binding intentions) of property at death

NMN
No middle name

Per Stirpes
Term meaning that the descendants of a beneficiary divide equally between them that portion of an estate which the beneficiary (i.e., their parent) would have taken if living; the share of the beneficiary filters down through succeeding generations

Personal Property
All property not considered real property

Probate
The act or process of proving a will (process wills go through for property to be distributed to beneficiaries)

Real Property
Land, buildings, houses and attached items such as fences and trees

Specific Bequest
A gift of specific personal property (everything but real estate) – i.e., a wedding ring

Statute
The written law

Testator/trix
The person making a will

Witness
One who, being present, personally testifies to an act or signature; an eyewitness

Thank You for Purchasing LawPak

Our goal is to design and develop the best in self-help legal materials.

Please remove this page from the booklet, complete the information below, fold and mail to LawPak. We will then be able to inform you of changes in the law within the next ninety days as these changes may affect the LawPak you purchased. This service is part of our continued commitment to you, the customer.

In addition, if you have encountered any new or additional information, forms, or processing procedures (not included in this publication) that you think would be helpful to others and should be incorporated into future LawPak editions, please take a few moments to send us the form and/or explain the procedure. We welcome your comments and suggestions.

name _____

address _____

city_____ state_____ zip_____

county _____ date of purchase _____

title of LawPak _____

place of purchase _____

Did you find the information in this book helpful? _____

Was it helpful and easy to use this book to accomplish your goals? (Circle one of each)

(very helpful)   1   2   3   4   5   6   (not at all)

(very easy)   1   2   3   4   5   6   (very difficult)

Comment and suggestions: _____

_____

_____

_____

_____

_____

_____

(Fold)

_____   Place
_____   Stamp
_____   Here

LawPak, Inc.
P.O. Box 221
Terrace Park, Ohio 45174

(Fold)

Other LawPak Affordable Legal Solutions

☐ Bankruptcy Chapter 7

This LawPak will assist the user in deciding if bankruptcy may be a legal solution to financial problems. Covers the topics of debts, property, and legal procedures, and includes the forms which are filed with the court to obtain a personal bankruptcy. Appropriate for single individuals or married couples.

$27.95 --

☐ Landlord/Tenant

This LawPak presents the legal obligations and rights of both the landlord and the tenant of residential property. Topics covered include security deposits, lease agreements, evictions, and liability for repairs or injury. Forms include a nine-page lease agreement, legal notices for evictions, and rental application.

$16.95 --

☐ Last Will and Testament

One of life's most neglected necessities is the Last Will and Testament. It allows *you* – not the state – to specify how you want your estate distributed upon your death, who you want to manage and oversee the distribution, and to whom you want to entrust the guardianship of your minor children. This LawPak covers provisions for determining beneficiaries, making specific bequests, appointing guardians for minor children, and naming executors for the estate. It is appropriate for anyone age 18 or older, regardless of marital status, whether or not they have minor children.

$16.25 --

☐ Living Will & Child's Medical Authorization

You can draft a Living Will to express in writing your preferences regarding the continuation or cessation of life-support efforts in the event you should become terminally ill — sparing loved ones the difficulty of making such decisions on your behalf. This LawPak also includes a Child's Medical Authorization form that parents can use to appoint other adults to make emergency health care decisions for their child when they, the parents, are not available.

$15.75 --

☐ Name Change

This LawPak allows the user to legally change an adult's or minor's name in the event of divorce, remarriage, adoption, errors in the birth certificate. It can also be used to select a name which is more appropriate to the user's personal preference. The publication includes the legal forms which are filed with the court to get the new name formally recognized by government agencies.

$15.95 --

☐ Ohio Dissolution of Marriage

There is a way to avoid the expense and time of using an attorney for a no-fault divorce. Thousands of couples have used this LawPak to obtain an Ohio Dissolution of Marriage. Among the topics it covers are: property, custody of minors, visitation rights, support, debts, and legal procedures. This publication contains the forms which are filed with the court to obtain a legal Ohio Dissolution.

$29.95 --

☐ Power of Attorney

By drafting this type of document, you can legally appoint another individual to act on your behalf. The authority you grant through this document may be broad (management of all financial affairs) or limited (sale of a home). This LawPak also contains a Durable Power of Attorney to appoint others to act on your behalf should you become incapacitated, thus avoiding guardianship/conservatorship court proceedings.

$14.95 --

☐ Real Estate Contracts (Buy & Sell)

Buying and selling a home may be the single most important financial transaction most consumer will ever make. LawPak's forms meet the requirements that make your real estate transactions legal and enforceable. A wide range of related topics and forms are included in this publication: real estate purchase contracts and contingencies, easement, land contracts, disclosure statements, option to purchase agreements, deeds and more.

$17.75 --

Three Ways to Order LawPak Publications

Mail order form with payment (check or money order) to:

LawPak, Inc., PO Box 221, Terrace Park OH 45174

Fax Credit Card Number with order form to:

1-513-831-1620

Call toll-free with credit card number to:

1-800-552-9725

- -

ORDER FORM

Ship to:

name _____

address _____

city _____ state _____ zip _____

telephone (_____) _____

TITLE	PRICE

* Shipping & handling
first-class shipping = $5.25
third-class shipping = $3.85
Add $15.00 to shipping cost for rush orders requiring overnight delivery.

subtotal $ _____

Ohio Sales Tax (6%) $ _____

shipping & handling* $ _____

TOTAL $ _____

Check one:

☐ Check or money order *(payable to LawPak)* enclosed.

☐ Charge to: ☐ MasterCard ☐ Visa

MAIL ORDER TO:
**LawPak, Inc.
PO Box 221
Terrace Park OH 45174**

card expiration date: ___ ___ / ___ ___   account # _____

signature _____